LETTERS OF HENRY VIII, 1526–29

∞⊷⊰⊱⊶∞

£2

uncovered editions

Series editor: Tim Coates

Other titles in the series

View these titles at www.uncovered-editions.co.uk

uncovered editions

LETTERS OF
HENRY VIII, 1526–29

EXTRACTS FROM THE CALENDAR OF
STATE PAPERS OF HENRY VIII

London: The Stationery Office

Applications for reproduction should be made in writing to The Stationery Office Limited, St Crispins, Duke Street, Norwich NR3 1PD.

ISBN 0 11 702453 8

First presented to Parliament in 1872 by J.S. Brewer as *The Calendar of State Papers of Henry VIII* as part of The Historical Manuscripts Commission.

A CIP catalogue record for this book is available from the British Library.

Combined cover photograph of Henry VIII by Holbein and historical document ©Hulton Getty (P58759 and P88246).

Typeset by J&L Composition Ltd, Filey, North Yorkshire.
Printed in the United Kingdom for The Stationery Office by Biddles Ltd, Guildford, Surrey.
TJ4079 C30 6/01

CONTENTS

About the series

Uncovered editions are historic official papers which have not previously been available in a popular form. The series has been created directly from the archive of The Stationery Office in London, and the books have been chosen for the quality of their story-telling. Some subjects are familiar, but others are less well known. Each is a moment in history.

About the series editor, Tim Coates

Tim Coates studied at University College, Oxford and at the University of Stirling. After working in the theatre for a number of years, he took up bookselling and became managing director, firstly of Sherratt and Hughes bookshops, and then of Waterstone's. He is known for his support for foreign literature, particularly from the Czech Republic. The idea for *uncovered editions* came while searching through the bookshelves of his late father-in-law, Air Commodore Patrick Cave OBE. He is married to Bridget Cave, has two sons, and lives in London.

Tim Coates welcomes views and ideas on the *uncovered editions* series. He can be e-mailed at tim.coates@theso.co.uk

EDITOR'S NOTE

The extracts in this book are taken from "The Calendar of State Papers of Henry VIII".

The original volumes that carry this title are part of a collection called "The Historical Manuscripts Commission", a remarkable project that was initiated in the reign of Queen Victoria and continues today. The purpose of the commission has always been to gather and republish original documents relating to the history of Britain.

The documents are sometimes copies, sometimes translations into modern English and sometimes descriptions of the apparent meaning of the original. It is as if the commissioner simply wished to provide the reader with the significance of what was found.

However, the published material never contained explanations or notes. No attempt has ever been made to give context or interpretation.

The royal papers move from subject to subject, as one would expect, in what is in effect a diary of government, and they have been gathered from sources in many countries.

Therefore this book needs to be read with this understanding of the origin of the material. In common with other titles in the series, it is not in any sense a complete history. It is, however, a collection of contemporary writings by those close to the events. The reader will need to seek other histories to obtain interpretation and elaboration, but what is here is, nevertheless, a clear portrait of one of the most astonishing moments in English history.

TIM COATES

April 2001

PERSONS

In England

HENRY VII (1457–1509), king from 1485

ELIZABETH, his queen

PRINCE ARTHUR (1486–1502), their elder son

HENRY VIII (1491–1547), their second son, king from 1509

MARGARET (1489–1541), their daughter, queen of James IV of Scotland (1503–13) and mother of James V, for whom she acted as regent

MARY (1495/6–1533), their daughter, married first to Louis XII of France (1514–15) and then to Charles Brandon, duke of Suffolk

KATHERINE OF ARAGON (1485–1536), married to Prince Arthur (November 1501 to April 1502) and following his death to Henry, and thus queen of England from 1509 to 1533; aunt of Charles V, king of Spain and Holy Roman Emperor

MARY (1516–1558), daughter of Henry VIII and Katherine of Aragon, queen of England and Ireland from 1553 to 1558

ANNE BOLEYN (OR BULLEN, c.1500/1–1536), daughter of Sir Thomas Boleyn by Elizabeth Howard, daughter of the duke of Norfolk; at the French court 1519–21 as lady-in-waiting to Queen Claude; second wife of Henry VIII from 1533 to 1536

THOMAS WOLSEY, CARDINAL (c.1475–1530), Henry VIII's chancellor (1515–29) and holder of the great seal, also archbishop of York and papal legate

SIR THOMAS MORE (1478–1535), succeeded Wolsey as Henry VIII's chancellor until 1532

THOMAS CROMWELL (*c*.1485–1540), earl of Essex, entered Wolsey's service in 1514 and became his agent and secretary; succeeded Sir Thomas More as Henry VIII's chancellor

JOHN FISHER (*c*.1469–1535), bishop of Rochester (1504–34), confessor to Katherine of Aragon and the only English bishop to oppose the invalidation of the marriage of Henry VIII and Katherine

CAMPEGGIO, CARDINAL, papal legate to the court of Henry VIII (initially in Rome, then in London)

DU BELLAY, bishop of Bayonne, ambassador from France

CHAPUYS, ambassador from Spain

INIGO DI MENDOZA, ambassador from Spain

In France

FRANCIS I (1494–1547), king of France from 1515; reign dominated by his rivalry with Charles V, which led to a series of wars (1521–26, 1528–29, 1536–38, 1542–44)

MARGARET OF SAVOY, daughter of Maximilian I (Holy Roman Emperor, 1459–1519) and Mary of Burgundy; married Philip II of Savoy (d. 1504); 1505 negotiations began (but failed) for marriage to Henry VII

MONTMORENCY, DUC DE (1493–1519), constable of France, made a marshal (1522) by Francis I; captured with Francis at Pavia (1525) and helped negotiate (1526) Francis's release

KNIGHT, ambassador from England

In Germany

SIR JOHN WALLOP, English noble

In Rome

POPE CLEMENT VII (1478–1534), allied himself with Francis I of France against the Holy Roman Emperor Charles V; was besieged by the Constable de Bourbon and for a while became his prisoner

JACOBO SALVIATI, CARDINAL, bishop of Verona, secretary to Pope Clement VII

SANGA, CARDINAL, secretary to Pope Clement VII

SS QUATUOR, CARDINAL, adviser to Pope Clement VII

CHARLES DE BOURBON (CONSTABLE DE BOURBON, 1490–1527), after losing favour with Francis I, concluded private alliance with Charles V and Henry VIII; made duke of Milan, commanded in northern Italy and killed while attacking Rome in 1527

SIR FRANCIS BRYAN
DR STEPHEN GARDINER
BRIAN TUKE
PETER VANNES
} ambassadors from Henry VIII in England

MAI, ambassador from Charles V in Spain

JOHN ANTHONY MUSCETULA, Imperial ambassador

In Spain

CHARLES V (1550–1558), king of Spain and Holy Roman Emperor; his defeat of Francis I in 1525 led to the formation of the Holy League against Charles by Pope Clement VII, Henry VIII, Francis I and the Venetians

ALMAIN, secretary to Charles V

GHINUCCI, bishop of Worcester
LEE
} ambassadors from England, initially in Rome, then in Spain

In Switzerland

DESIDERIUS ERASMUS (1466–1536), philosopher, writer, academic

In Venice

SIR GREGORY CASALE
PAUL CASALE
VINCENT CASALE
} ambassadors to the *Signory* from England

SELECTED GLOSSARY

advocation	revocation; recalling of the cause for consideration in Rome
arrect	apportion
attemper	moderate
bartlage	preparation of stone or wood
breve	a papal brief; a less formal papal document than a bull
bull	an edict of the pope with his seal affixed
burgalett	apartment
Caesarians	supporters of the Holy Roman Emperor
common	to share, to discuss
common weal	well-being, interest and prosperity of the country
consistory	papal council
contumacious, contumax	showing wilful disobedience of the law
debellation	defeat
demore	damage
elengenes	longing
en gambades	in kind
entendement	agreement
femerall	outlet for smoke in a roof
Fleet	London gaol until 1842; on the River Fleet

forsan	perhaps
glose	gloss, for appearance
had liever	had rather
halpace	a kneeling place, an altar
Hanaper	former department of Chancery
herdhewer	stonecutter
Imperialists	Spanish and German armies of the Holy Roman Empire
indited	composed
jusques au foye	in good faith
lanzknecht	landsknecht; mercenary footsoldier of the 16th century
League	alliance of English, French, papal and Venetian troops
Marrans	Moors or Jews, from Spain
monition	a formal ecclesiastical warning
muidz	measure, of grain etc.
paynim	heathen
praemunire	asserting papal jurisdiction in England (in the case of Wolsey); later: disputing the religious supremacy of the king
promotor	coadjutor
proveditor	inspector or commissioner, especially in Republic of Venice
recusation	objection, appeal
referendary	court official who was the medium of communication with the pope, emperor etc.
regrater	one who buys and sells again in or near the same market, thus raising the price
schawm	musical instrument, a predecessor of the oboe
seneschal	steward

signatura	papal audience, specifically for the signing of documents
Signory	council of the city-state of Venice
tabret	drum
tours de corde	twists of the rope
transumpt	a legally authorised copy
waywode	vaivode, Hungarian general

These letters and papers are from a collection of reports on the state papers of Henry VIII, prepared for and presented to the British parliament in 1872 by J.S. Brewer. This selection covers a period of just over three years, from the summer of 1526 to the autumn of 1529.

Europe at that time was ruled by a small number of dynastic families who were accustomed, for the sake of their own security, to the fighting of wars and the creation of balances of power, sometimes in battle, sometimes by devious diplomacy and often by the strategic marriages of their children. Holding power was a continuous and dangerous endeavour. Yet, in many ways, this was one of the most civilised and creative times in history. Rarely has there been a period of more concentrated artistic excellence and achievement, in painting, sculpture, architecture, lawmaking, music and literature. Among the great patrons of these arts were the same ruling families.

A thousand years of unquestioned certainty and dependence upon the Catholic Church as the foundation of all society were coming to an end. Doubt and dislike of corruption had caused the rise of a Protestant movement articulated by Martin Luther, which challenged the divine authority and hierarchy of the pope in Rome and added an extra dimension to the distribution of popular power. Throughout Europe, the Reformation of the Church had begun.

By 1526 Henry VIII and Katherine of Aragon—aunt of Charles V, the king of Spain and Holy Roman Emperor— had ruled England for over 16 years. Henry owed his sovereignty to his father's success in English civil war, to his marriage and to his subsequent political sagacity. Indeed, with the help of Katherine and Wolsey, his chief minister, he had proved himself a worthy monarch, esteemed among his peers.

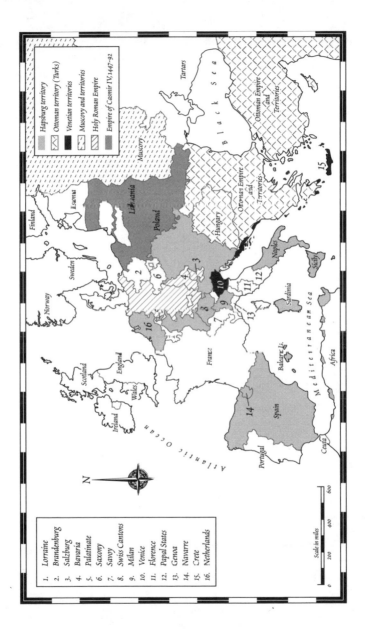

Hapsburg territory	(light stipple pattern)
Ottoman territory (Turks)	(hatched pattern)
Venetian territories	(black)
Muscony and territories	(dotted pattern)
Holy Roman Empire	(diagonal line pattern)
Empire of Casmir IV, 1447–92	(grey)

1. Lorraine
2. Brandenburg
3. Salzburg
4. Bavaria
5. Palatinate
6. Saxony
7. Savoy
8. Swiss Cantons
9. Milan
10. Venice
11. Florence
12. Papal States
13. Genoa
14. Navarre
15. Crete
16. Netherlands

N

Scale in miles

0   200   400   600

Atlantic Ocean

Mediterranean Sea

Black Sea

Portugal
Spain
Ceuta
Africa
Balearic Is.
Sardinia
Sicily
Naples
France
Savoy
Hungary
Ottoman Empire and Territories
Tartars
Muscony
Poland
Lithuania
Finland
Sweden
Norway
Scotland
Ireland
Wales
England

AUGUST 1526 TO MARCH 1527

In September 1526 a Spanish army of mercenaries was invading Italy. Though not directly instructed by Charles V, the Spanish king, they had his support, and they were moving close to Rome. A "League", an alliance of English, French, papal and Venetian troops, was fighting against the Spanish and German armies of the Holy Roman Empire, the "Imperialists".

At the same time Hungary was invaded by Turkey and this seemed to threaten the peace of the whole of Europe. The pope called for all Christendom to unite against the infidel. In particular, he turned to Henry VIII and his chancellor, Cardinal Wolsey, who were both distinguished in their support for the

Church against the Protestant calls for reform led by Martin Luther.

For more than a decade Wolsey had been Henry's chief minister, managing both foreign and domestic policy with great skill.

Erasmus to Francis (physician to Cardinal Wolsey)

Is often astonished why England is so frequently visited with the plague. Thinks that much is due to the construction of the houses, which are so full of windows as to admit the light and exclude the air. Complains of the chalk floors and the rushes, which are so carelessly renewed that the bottom layer remains sometimes 20 years, harbouring all sorts of nastiness of men and dogs and offal. Thinks also that the cause is to be found in the abundance of salt water, marsh grounds and the like, and the salt diet of the people. Thirty years ago if I had entered a chamber which had not been inhabited for some months, I caught a fever. Wishes the streets were kept more clean from mud and other abominations. Would have written to the cardinal, but had no time. (August 1526)

Campeggio to Henry VIII

The pope, who is in great trouble, is sending to England the bishop of Worcester to inform the king of recent occurrences at which he was present. All his hope at this critical time is in the king. All Christendom is in danger from the Turk, now that the king of Hungary has been defeated and slain. (Rome, 24 September 1526)

Sir John Wallop to Wolsey

Has sent a servant of his with letters dated September 30. Has heard from a merchant who was in Ovo when the battle happened, and came thence on the 12th ult. with particulars of the battle. The king of Hungary was

encamped with 50,000 men on a hill on this side of the
Duno; the Turk on the other side had concealed his ordnance near the river and sent over 5,000 or 6,000 men to
skirmish, firing a few small guns that the Hungarians
might think he had no other. The Turks were overthrown,
and a bigger company was then sent with orders to attack
the Hungarians on the hill, retreat towards the concealed
artillery, and then open, so that they might be in the very
face of the shot. The Turk with his band also retired, so that
the Hungarians might think there was no danger. This was
carried out; many of the Hungarians were slain by the
artillery, but they immediately rallied, and seeing the Turks
still flee thought that the shot was all past and that they
could set upon them before the guns were recharged. The
rest of the guns were then fired, and the Hungarians
utterly broken. The Turk, with all his power, then set upon
them, and if night had not come on few or none would
have escaped. The king was slain. The Turk is lord over all
Hungary and has burnt the Austrian frontier, which seems
to imply that he will withdraw in the winter; but, by the
enclosed copy of a letter from the archduke to the bishop
of Cologne, Wolsey will perceive the contrary. The Turk
has 20,000 lanzknechts with double wages. He will allow
the people to continue in their belief, paying only half the
duties they formerly paid to their king. His ordnance is
above 800 great pieces, as well as the small. The archduke
has gone from Innsbruck towards the Austrian frontier.

Thinks the king of Hungary must have had bad espial
to allow the Turk's ordnance to be placed undiscovered, or
else he had little experience. (Cologne on the Rhine, 9
October 1526)

Wolsey to Henry VIII

I have received news from the foreign ambassadors who
were here with me that the League has taken Cremona,

and Genoa is expected to surrender in five or six days. Francis I is extremely displeased with the detestable attempts of Cardinal Colonna and Hugh de Moncada against the pope. Urges the king to give the pope, for the maintenance of 5,000 Swiss and 400 men-at-arms, 30,000 or 35,000 ducats, by which he may forbear to enter the League and mediate more effectually with the emperor. The French king and the Venetians will bear a similar charge. King Henry will secure peace, have the gratitude of the pope and the League, save his treasure, preserve his amity with the emperor; and thus, by his wise counsel, Christendom may attend to the debellation of the Turks. Wishes to have the king's instructions. Sends letters received from Francis. (Hampton Court, 9 October 1526)

Campeggio to Wolsey

Was greatly pleased, on the arrival of Cardinal Sanga, to hear of Wolsey's good health. They have much confidence in the king as the author of peace between Christian princes, and the champion of the liberty of Christendom. The pope's thoughts are all concentrated on the means of defending the Lord's flock committed to his charge. The fleet of the Spanish viceroy is hourly expected from Spain, and if it comes and finds the pope unprepared, total ruin will ensue. The army of the confederates has compelled Cremona to surrender, and is now laying siege to Milan and Genoa. (Rome, 22 October 1526)

J.M. Giberto, bishop of Verona, to Wolsey

The news by Sanga would have given them greater hopes if it had not arrived when his Holiness did not look for hope, but results. Had aid arrived in time, as his Holiness desired, the pride of the enemy would not have increased to such an unheard of extent as to threaten the pope's destruction. He hopes, however, that the king's aid will now flow more fully the longer it has been restrained, and he doubts not that the king and Wolsey will be greatly incensed at the injuries done to the pope, the Church and God himself. The safety or destruction of Italy depends upon the king. They are closely pressed and cannot wait much longer, and therefore the pope anxiously expects letters from England as soon as the king shall have heard the wrongs he endures. If aid does not come speedily it will be of no use, as Wolsey will probably have heard fully already from Gambara. He is pleased to hear Sanga's confirmation of Wolsey's good wishes, expressed not only by his word but also his countenance. Is grateful to find that Wolsey remembers him, and often speaks of him, and will take care to satisfy their wishes in all things. (22 October 1526)

Henry VIII to Pope Clement VII

Greatly regrets the evils of the times. Could not help shedding tears on reading the pope's breve of 22 September. Wept over the loss of Hungary, which is owing to the dissensions of Christendom. When other princes have agreed, he will not be behindhand in joining the crusade. Exhorts the pope to bear up, trusting that the danger will disperse. Desires credence for Gregory Casale. (Westminster, 23 October 1526)

Lee to Wolsey

News came on the 18th that Cardinal Colonna and Hugh de Moncada had entered Rome on 20 September and spoiled the pope's palace with the "burgalett" adjoining. The pope fled to Castle Angelo. Hears that the emperor is "marvellously sorry that they have done so". Has not been to court for 14 days. (24 October 1526)

Lee to Henry VIII

Wrote in his last by way of Bilbao of Moncada's entrance into Rome and the flight of the pope. Since then, news has come of the spoiling of St Peter's. Some write that the soldiers put the copes upon their backs and mitres on their heads, which savoured more of paynims than of good Christian men. The emperor takes the matter very heavily, and offers to make amends. The said Hugh de Moncada, as they report here, is a hardy man and hath good skill in the war; but few things have hitherto proved well in his hands, and this they account a great blot. The pope has sent hostages and made an abstinence of war with him for four months. Moncada has agreed to withdraw his army to Naples. Is informed that the pope has sent to the emperor for confirmation of Moncada's set.

News has come from those about Bourbon that Milan cannot hold out for lack of victuals. The nuncio writes that on 29 August the king of Hungary at daybreak gave the Turk battle with 25,000 men. He fled from the field with a knight and a gentleman of his chamber, and as he was proceeding to cross the stream of the Danube "his horse, being sore wounded in the battle, fell under him, and he overcome with poiz of his armour could no wise help himself. The knight seeing that, leapt off his horse to the intent to help the king, but remedy was none. They were both drowned together. Our Lord pardon their souls! The king did valiant sets in the battle. This telleth the gentleman of his chamber." Does not believe the report that he escaped, as the queen eight days after could hear nothing of him, his chancellor or his council, all of whom are supposed to have perished. Very few escaped.

The next day the Turk burst Monox. It was supposed he would have gone to Buda. The queen fled at midnight to Possonia. By the king's death, Bohemia falls to Don

Ferdinand. The pope intends to visit Barcelona, and desires to meet Wolsey and the emperor. Caesar, chief esquire, is to be sent ambassador to the pope, to excuse the violence at Rome and punish the robbers, but also to express the emperor's intention to visit his Holiness and save him so troublesome a journey. (Granada, 1 November 1526)

Translation of the New Testament

Mandate of the archbishop of Canterbury to John Voysey, bishop of Exeter, to search for English translations of the New Testament, as containing heretical pravity. (Lambeth, 3 November 1526)

A list of the books prohibited:

The Supplication of Beggars
The Revelation of Antichrist of Luther
The New Testament of Tindall
The Wicked Mammon
The Obedience of a Christian Man
An Introduction to Paul's Epistle to the Romans
A Dialogue betwixt the Father and the Son
Oeconomiae Christianae
Unio Dissiedentium
Piae Precationes
Captivatas Babilonica
Johannes Hus in Oseam
Zuinglius in Catabaptistas
De Pueris Instituendis
Brentius de Administranda Republica
Lutherus ad Galatas
De Libertate Christiana
Luther's Exposition upon the Pater Noster

Campeggio to Wolsey

There is fear of war everywhere; for since the sack of St Peter's and the palace, it is said that the viceroy is coming with a strong fleet to occupy Italy. The Imperialists are encouraged thereby. The pope is enlisting soldiers and recalling his troops from the siege of Milan. He already has 6,000 Italian foot, 3,000 Swiss, 400 men-at-arms and 1,200 light horse. They are stationed in these towns which are held by the Colonnese from the Church. The Neopolitans are also said to be preparing forces, and they are expecting the arrival of the fleet. It is not known whether it has left Carthagena, and Peter Navarre has gone to meet it with a strong fleet of the allies. Genoa has been besieged by the allies for three months, is pressed by want and will probably soon be reduced. Milan is surrounded by a slow rather than an active blockade. There is thus no hope of peace except in the king, especially as it is reported that the emperor has said he will refer the whole matter to him, and the king of France and the other allies will do the same. (Rome, 6 November 1526)

Campeggio to Wolsey

Thanks him for his letters of the 18 October. Is glad to find that his services are acceptable to the king, and will henceforth allow no courier to leave without a letter. In the consistory this day the pope expressed his satisfaction at the professions of the king, and his promise to send a considerable sum of money for defending the Church's dignity. The king is truly *defensor fidei*. It has been resolved to put up a monition against those who a few days ago attacked and plundered St Peter's and the palace. (Rome, 7 November 1526)

Roman news

A spy who left Florence on 1 November reports that the pope made an agreement with the Germans on the 31 October, promising them 150,000 ducats, out of which two months' wages were to be paid in hand and the rest in three months. He was also to pay the Spaniards 100,000 ducats, and had promised them to make three Neapolitan cardinals, one of whom is of the family of Caraffa, and to deliver to them the city of Castellana and the castle of Forli, and to confirm to them Ostia and Civitavecchia. Hostages were given in the house of Cardinal Colonna, but under the guard of Germans. The Spaniards and the Germans were constantly falling out, with bloodshed and robbery on both sides. In four days the army was to depart from Rome, no one knew whither. The infantry were unruly. Fabricius Marcimanus has obtained the state of Santo Paulo, Sanctum Restum and Castrum Novum. They were pillaging everything they could, and threatened to return to Rome. The said Fabricius has 22 banners, with 30 foot soldiers under each. The foot soldiers of the League who were in Castellana were lying in wait for two of Fabricius' banners which were going towards Stabia. (In the hand of Vannes. 7 November 1526)

The navy

An abstract of the daily charges for the king's ships yet remaining, the 16th day of November in the 18th year of his reign:

Estimate for a year's wages for mariners to keep the following ships, and for the number of cables that each will consume:

Henry Grace à Dieu: 8 mariners to keep her, at 4*l*. 6*s*. 8*d*. a month, counting 13 months to the year.

Mary Rose: for 8 mariners to keep her, 4*l*. 12*s*. 8*d* a month;
    for 6 cables, 42*l*.

Gabriel Royal: for 10 mariners, 114*s*. 4*d*.; for 8 cables, 80*l*.

Peter Pomegarnard: 6 mariners, 72*s*. a month; 6 cables, 42*l*.

Great Bark: 4 mariners, 46*s*. 8*d*.; 6 cables, 30*l*.

Less Bark: 3 mariners, 36*s*. 8*d*.; 4 cables, 20*l*.

Great Galley: one mariner, 10*s*. 4*d*.

Mary George: one mariner, 10*s*. 4*d*.; 2 cables, 10*l*.

Kateryn Galley: 1 mariner, 10*s*. 4*d*.; 2 cables, 6*l*. 13*s*. 4*d*.

Swepestakes 1 mariner, 10*s*. 4*d*.; 2 cables, 6*l*. 13*s*. 4*d*.

Swallow: 1 mariner, 10*s*, 4*d*.; 2 cables, 6*l*.

Total for one year 568*l*. 15*s*. 2*d*.

The *Mynyon* and the *Mary Gylford* are not yet come from
Bordeaux, so their charges are not put down. The expense
of maintaining the great ships' dock at Portsmouth, and
caulking all the said ships, cannot well be estimated. (16
November 1526. A paper roll)

Proposals for a treaty between England and France

The king of England desires a perpetual peace between
France and England, and to that end will satisfy the French
king and his successors for all the rights he claims or pos-
sesses in France. He will give his only daughter, Mary, in
marriage, with a suitable dower and jewels, to the French
king, making her heir to the throne, if there be no sons
born subsequently. In event of her not coming to the
throne, he will give her as much as the emperor had with
his wife, or as much as was promised to the emperor as her
portion in the late treaty. The French king to bind himself
and his successors to pay a certain amount of salt and
money, etc., annually to Henry and his successors, through
the French king and his daughter, but it is not to be considered as a tribute. In any case security will be given for
the amount of the princess's dowry. If there are no children

to succeed from this marriage this agreement to be void, and all treaties and conventions to be as they are now. In all cases the present treaty is to remain. Henry will enter into a treaty with the French king for the restoration, by force or otherwise, of his children detained by the emperor as hostages.★

The University of Oxford to Wolsey

In praise of the unprecedented encouragement given to letters by Wolsey, especially in the foundation of the new college, a work which would have been magnificent even if no more highly adorned than was intimated by the bishop of Lincoln; for he said there were to be about 200 scholars. The magnificence of the occasion transcends their power of description, and they have requested the bishop to report what took place. But they understand Wolsey has now resolved to augment the salaries of all the fellows, and to establish seven lectureships, for which he will engage learned men from foreign countries; and that all the schools are about to be built at his own cost. If so, they will consider him no longer as the founder of a college but of the university itself. The masters (*rectores et praesides*) have arranged a scheme of hours and places for the lectures, which Robert Carter will present to him.

Francis I and Princess Mary

A speech addressed to Henry VIII in commendation of the proposed marriage of his daughter to Francis I:

The orator extols Henry's personal qualifications (*fortunae dotibus principe dignis, heroica corporis majestate, venerando vultu, aspectu et pro dignitalis certe ratione minime formidabili, bellicis denique virtutibus*) and his defence of orthodoxy

---

★ The French king's children had been taken prisoner by the Imperial army.

against Luther, on whom he had inflicted such wounds that he had driven him almost to fury. For the defence of the Faith he has been reconciled to Francis, and he may wage war against the enemies of Christ by the sword as he has done by his writings. He has always sought peace in war, and never swerved from the object of promoting the true Faith. He has undergone incredible labours in reconciling the differences of others, regarding the Turk as the only enemy. Henry will put the finishing stroke to his services in behalf of the Faith by giving his daughter in marriage to the most Christian king.

Petition of the bakers of London to Wolsey as chancellor
They have always been accustomed to "occupy" the making and selling of bread for the city, according to acts of parliament and the city customs; and since the time of Edward II they have been used to take up wheat arriving in London, at the prices given them by the mayor; but, within the last five years (by the decree of the mayor and council in 1521) certain persons, aldermen and others, out of malice to the mystery, and "under colour of a common weal", procured that all the wheat coming to the city should be brought to the Bridgehouse, taken up at the mayor's price, and there garnered, and that the bakers should not be allowed to buy any other wheat but this. Articles were drawn up by the mayor, aldermen and bridgemasters, binding the bakers to do this, which articles are ready to be shown to your grace. By this scheme the providers of the wheat gain yearly 1,733*l*. 6*s*. 8*d*. at the expense of the bakers and the commonalty. They sent an answer to this effect to John Brigges, then mayor. Last year they were compelled to take out of the Bridgehouse 2,000 qrs. of musty and unwholesome wheat at 13*s*. 5*d*. a qr. to make bread of, by which they "fell in great slander" amongst the commons, who said that the musty bread

caused great infection and sickness. Persons have also been sent into divers shires to buy wheat at 7s. or 8s. a qr., whereas, before their coming, it might have been bought for 6s. or 6s. 8d., "which seemeth more to use the order of regraters than to be governors of a good common weal". Lately the mayor and aldermen tried to compel them to buy 2,000 qrs. of musty wheat at 12s. when sweet wheat may be bought for 7s. or 8s. When some bakers refused, the mayor sent them to Newgate for 11 days and shut up their houses and shops, not allowing their wives or families to visit them or sell their bread. They have in vain asked the mayors for the last five years for redress for these and other injuries, and have been continually rebuked, imprisoned and wronged; and now ask Wolsey for some remedy that they may have sufficient living, and not be utterly undone. (Headed: To the most reverend father in God, Thomas Lord Cardinal and Legate, archbp. of York, primate and chancellor of England)

Italy: Ex literis Prothonotarii Casalii

The continuation of the war rests with the pope, who will be firm for it if he is strengthened by the French king. It is thought that the Venetians will not consent to the duchy of Milan being given to Bourbon. Great part of the Imperial soldiers have left Milan, and have cruelly laid waste most of the country. It is thought if the Spaniards leave, the duke of Milan will come with a force strong enough to resist the Germans, though Louis de Bellejoyeuse remains there with 3,000 foot. If the Spaniards go towards Tuscany, the Venetians will follow them, and destroy them by starvation without fighting. The Florentines, through fear, will not prove equal to the occasion; but by letters to the captain of the Germans, intercepted by Bourbon, it appears they are preparing to attack Piacenza, which is well fortified. It is reported that a nobleman, head of the faction of Sforza, has entered Novara, and hopes it will be defended by his faction.

The pope, notwithstanding what was said by his ambassador in France to the bishops of Bath and Worcester, will gladly consent that Milan should be placed in the king's hands. It was reported that the Germans had crossed two rivers, one beyond Fiorenzuola, the other beyond Piacenza, and that they were going towards Pavia. It was supposed that the Germans had left Pavia to protect those who had crossed the Po. Colonna's party are neglecting their affairs. The viceroy has not yet left Gaeta. The pope advises the king not to assist the archduke against the waywode, lest he be compelled to turn for assistance to the Turk, but rather to persuade the waywode to treat, and the archduke to give him his sister in marriage, who he has already asked. It is said that Renzo brings no money, as was hoped, but says it was long ago sent by the Swiss. It is a question whether the French king has not recalled it, suspecting an agreement between the pope and the viceroy, and resolved on a different course.

The archbishop of Capua has sent fearful news, and a nephew of the general with the capitulation, of which an abstract is enclosed, to show the exorbitant demands of the viceroy. Much deceit is visible in the archbishop's letters. He writes also that the duke of Ferrara has been appointed captain-general in Italy by the emperor, and that he will assume the office in three days. The pope had determined to send Renzo to Abruzzi, and D. Orazio (Baglione) to Naples, through the March of Ancona, to join the fleet in an attempt against the viceroy; but as he has no money but what he receives from the king, he cannot do either. The pope is firmly resolved to defend himself as long as he can, and it is arranged that France shall take up the matter in earnest. Guido Rangoni writes that the Spaniards are in great straits for money. The emperor is striving cunningly for universal monarchy. Let France and others look to it. It is the common opinion that only one way remains to crush the Imperialists, by attacking them vigorously in their extreme necessity. This would require 300,000 cr. The pope has sent back the ambassador of the duke of Urbino to learn the state of affairs there, and what the duke will do if the Germans turn upon Rome and Tuscany, which could not be remedied unless the duke joined the French forces and pursued them. The pope sends to him because the Venetians entrust in great measure their military affairs to him, and he has got the Venetians to send a secretary to encourage the Florentines. They will send troops to Polesii against the duke of Ferrara, and the pope into Romagna, if he is strong enough, for he fears lest Ferrara join the Germans in Reggio, and carry them pay. (In the hand of Vannes. 5 January 1527)

Campeggio to Wolsey

Expresses the satisfaction he felt when he first had the happiness of being personally introduced to Wolsey, his thanks for the care Wolsey has taken of his interests, and especially for his late letters, when Campeggio had fallen into some disgrace with the king, for which there was no foundation. Has now been able to throw aside all trouble, and can sleep safe from fear of detraction. Cannot express the delight with which the consistory heard from the pope that the king had sent him an ambassador (Russell), who had arrived from Civitavecchia with a large sum of money, and, in order to display his liberality to the Holy See, had received orders from the king to denounce war against the viceroy and Bourbon if they did not forthwith abandon the siege of different cities of the Church. The cardinals are unanimous in declaring that Henry was God's blessing to them, the patron of Italian liberty, and the real defender of the Faith.

Praises the king's book against Luther highly, which, he says, is to show that he can defend Christendom not less by genius and learning than by money and arms. (Rome, 7 February 1527)

Italy

Arrangement between Francis I and the Venetians for carrying on the war in Italy; consisting of 17 articles.

It is agreed that 30,000 Swiss, Germans, French and Italians shall be kept in pay, comprehending the foot serving under the marquis of Saluzzo. The month to commence on May 15. Arrangements for the pay on both sides.

Efforts shall be made to induce the duke of Ferrara to join the League; in which event he shall be appointed *generalissimo*. Francis, duke of Milan, to contribute, if possible. Money to be sent to Renzo, if desirable, to carry on the war in the Neapolitan territory. Arrangements for the fleet under the command of Peter of Navarre. Neither party to make terms with the emperor apart. Liberty to be granted to the king of England to act as mediator. Nothing in this treaty to affect the former league, as regards Henry VIII and the cardinal.

Herman Rynge to Henry VIII

Trusts that the king already knows that he has fulfilled his orders. Has sent to the king a barrel of powdered wild boar venison from the bishop of Cologne, and also six barrels of preserved lampreys, such as the Emperor Maximilian had from him every Lent. It has been prepared only by his wife and daughters.

The Archduke Ferdinand, who is crowned king of Bohemia, and writes himself king of Hungary, has sent hither for men and powder to be at Vienna on St George's day. It is thought that if they wait for the diet to be held at

Ravelsberghe, the Turk might have entered so far as to endanger Hungary and the neighbouring realms. Thinks Ferdinand has written likewise to other lords and cities of the empire. The messenger has today gone to Thistildorp [Düsseldorf], where the duke of Saxony marries the eldest daughter of the duke of Gulycke. Thinks that they will come hither in a few days, at the desire of the bishop of Cologne. (Cologne, 2 March 1527)

APRIL 1527 TO EARLY JULY 1527

The marriage between Henry VIII and Katherine of Aragon was arranged by his parents when he was 12. They had previously arranged a marriage between Katherine and Henry's elder brother Arthur, but Arthur died only a few months after the wedding. The marriage was important for Henry's father, as the throne of England had been won in battle and needed to be secured by dynastic alliance. The king of England could now always call upon the Spanish for support in the face of challenge.

However, after nearly 20 years the couple had failed to produce a surviving son. The succession may once again be contested in civil war on Henry's death, and this was a serious concern to

both Henry and his advisers. Moreover, Henry, who had had several mistresses, was now attracted to Anne Boleyn.

Henry seeks the views of theologians. Dispensation had been
granted by Pope Julius at the time of the second marriage on the
grounds that Arthur and Katherine were married for a short time
and were not intimate, due to Arthur's sickness. Henry is proposing that the dispensation should not have been granted as
Katherine was previously married to his brother, that the marriage
is illegal and that they should be divorced.

Lee to Wolsey

As the emperor's answer was short, went to Almain to
complain of it. He said, "We must maintain the authority
of our ambassador, and leave something to him". I said,
"You give us no answer touching your secret instructions". He said that the emperor put his whole trust in the
king and Wolsey and that if the latter would serve him all
would be right. "But you must beware that you trust not
the French king too much; for he mocketh you as he hath
done us." On this he plucked out of his bosom a letter
received out of France the night before, written by Perot,
the orator in France, containing these words:

> The French king said to me, "The king of England would
> have me to take his daughter, and give him Boleyn. Nay,
> nay! The cardinal wrote to me, desiring and most instantly
> beseeching me that, for a continuance of new amity
> between the king of England and me, I should send my
> orators into England, and give them mandatum to
> common and conclude there; and, to colour the thing, that
> I should ask the daughter of England. But I had much
> liever that the emperor would send a gentleman hither,
> that we may common our matters among ourselves; for I
> would not have it concluded at the king of England's

hands. They say in England that I shall come thither, and
that all the triumph is prepared for the French king. True it
is, for it is for the duke of Richmond, whom they intend
to make king of Ireland; and that at length he shall be for
the French king, as Scotland is."

He further said that Francis would not give us a foot of
land nor marry the princess. Some of this he said by word
of mouth. He said that Francis was hated by his subjects,
and did not dare come to Paris. (Valladolid, 8 April 1527)

Campeggio to Henry VIII

The defence of your majesty against Luther, which has
lately reached us, has given great satisfaction. The pope has
ordered a large impression of it. (Rome, 10 April 1527)

Italy

Extracts from letters of the prothonotary Casale:

The ambassador of the duke of Milan in France
writes to his master of the good offices of the legate
Wolsey towards him, and of the preparations made by the
king of England. States that the marriage is to be concluded by the French king or his son within the year; that
the king of England is bound to take up arms for the
delivery of the French king's children in June, and, in case
the French king changes his mind about the princess, he
is bound to pay the costs of the war and 50,000 cr. annually; and that there are other articles about salt and mutual
intercourse. The French king would not accept the justi-
fication of the pope by his nuncio, but told him that was
not the way to procure peace. If the Venetians see the
pope is really willing to defend himself and fight, they
will assist him; but they will not put their troops in peril
on uncertain words, nor favour him who deserted them.
If the Imperialists were moderately resisted, they could

not be in a worse position than the present. (Venice, 15 April 1527)

Campeggio to Wolsey

The pope has been compelled to change his intentions of sending the bishop of Verona to England. When Bourbon and the Germans were informed of the arrangement between the pope and the viceroy they opposed it, and, treating it with contempt, burned the towns in Bologna and plundered everywhere; then, advancing into Tuscany, and camping 12 miles from Florence, they intended, when that was done, to lay siege to Rome. The pope has been compelled to put himself on the defensive. His enemies are partly Lutherans and partly Marrans, who care as much to destroy religion itself as to trample on Italy. Hopes the king will defend them. These letters will be presented by Russell. Has an attack of the gout. (Rome, 28 April 1527)

The sack of Rome

On Saturday 4th May 1527 Bourbon arrived before Rome, and asked the pope's consent to his passing to Naples, offering to pay for provisions. He received a rough refusal from Signor Rans, at the instigation of the pope, who had received for recruiting his army 300,000 ducats by creating eight new cardinals. On Sunday the 5th Bourbon drew off his troops from Rome behind St Peter's, pretending to cross the Tiber; but early on Monday the 6th, whilst there was a great mist, he prepared to assault the town behind the Campo Santo at Thurion Gate, and Sicur was among the first to mount the walls, where four ensigns were planted. He was there wounded, assisted to descend, and carried into a neighbouring chapel, but when the gate of Thurion was taken he was conveyed to the church of Campo Santo. Captain Rans, who was on the wall with 4,000 men, seeing that they retreated, as many men were killed by the artillery of the assailants, cried out the Bourbon, Orange and four ensigns were taken, in order to encourage them to return to the wall. They, however, retreated to the Place St Esprit; but Rans left them and went to the Castle of Sant'Angelo, where was the pope, with five or six cardinals. Cardinals SS Quatuor, who was wounded, and Ezis retired with Rans. The besiegers continued to advance; and the Romans, seeing that Rans had deserted them, tried to escape, some jumping into the Tiber. The Imperialists killed every one they met—men, women, and children. This lasted from the morning to 2.0, during which time Bourbon was killed. Before his death he confessed, received his Creator, and desired to be carried into Milan, though some think that he meant Rome, for he was continually saying "à Rome, à Rome". About two in the afternoon, the Imperialists took the gate of St Pancras, where they encountered some resistance, and then began to pillage, which lasted at least 10 or 12 days, without there being any resistance, except in three or four houses which they mined and blew up. Many people had sent their goods, amounting to two millions of gold, to the house of the Portuguese ambassador, but they were obliged to surrender on promise of their lives. They gave out that as soon as the city was taken, the prince of Orange took possession of the pope's palace, in which were lodged cardinals Campeggio, Cibo and Rodulpho, "et le ... Jehan d'Urbin, capitaine des Espagnaers en la chancelle[rie] ... maison du duc de Millan". Both the generals tried to stop the pillage, but unsuccessfully, though afterwards the Germans obeyed the prince, and the Spaniards Captain D'Urbin. On May 19th the pope was still in Sant'Angelo. Before the taking of the city, the viceroy of Naples and the pope had made a truce for eight months, during which both armies were to retire; a viceroy went with the pope's maître d'hôtel to persuade Bourbon and the Imperial officers to retreat also, but they took it ill, and told him not to interfere with their affairs. It was reported that the maître d'hôtel was wounded. The viceroy was obliged to retire to Naples, where he was on the 19th.

Negotiations were carried on between the pope and the deputies of the prince of Orange, and it is agreed that his Holiness shall pay 300,000 ducats; the cardinals with him, who are De Monte, Farnesse, SS Quatuor, Pizano, Trivolze, Besine, Campeggio, Ancona, Cesis, la Minerve, St Egedio and, it is said, Ara Coeli, 200,000 ducats; and certain merchants who were with them, 100,000 ducats; that the pope and eight cardinals shall go as the emperor's prisoners to Gaeta, and surrender Ostia, Civitavecchia, Parma, Placentia and Lucca; and that Cardinal Colonna, who entered four days after the capture, with 8,000 men, shall be vice-pope. "Lequel De Calonne se mist au pallaix St Gep ... de Campeflore, et sont avecq luy les Cardin[aulx de] Tortosa et Trefort, De Laval, De Ezarinne (Caesarinus), Sene, et T ...", who, though they were good Imperialists, have redeemed their houses at the following sums: the cardinal of Tortosa for 40,000 ducats; De Laval, 45,000 ducats; De Ezarinne, 35,000; De Sene, 40,000; and De Tarobanche, 25,000. After paying these ransoms, their houses were again plundered, and they have been obliged to retire with Cardinal Colonna.

Meanwhile, the army of the League had been reinforced, and put in order to march against Rome. The pope was informed thereof by means of a disguised page, and broke off the treaty. They arrived on 2nd May, and are at L''Insula, four miles from Rome, numbering 30,000, but they have great fear of the Imperialists. Provisions are dear at Rome; but there cannot be great want, as the League cannot prevent the arrival of victuals from Naples. The pope was not taken on May 19th, and it is said that he has victuals for five or six months. News came to Ligorne on June 3rd that he was not taken.

The Florentines, on hearing of the taking of Rome, drove out the Medicis and made a *Signory* like that at Venice, and have sent governors to Pisa and Leghorn to govern in their name, and not in that of the pope; but the castles still hold out for the Medicis.

The Great Chancellor of the Emperor has been sent to Italy with 30,000 ducats and other commissions. "La Regente, la Reyne de Navare, apelle dame d'Alanson, Mons.Vandome, le Carenal (mal volu) de Lorrayne, Mons, de Lottrecht et le Chansyler." The viceroy has written to the 'Emperor' [in cipher] to come himself, "other in good time to make p. [peace]" or else there is no possibility of keeping Italy longer.

Italy

From the letters of the *Signory* of Venice:

The proveditor of Pisa writes on the 10th from Deruta that the enemy entered Rome on the 6th and plundered it, that Bourbon was killed by a musket and that 3,000 German foot were slain.

The pope and cardinals, except Valla and Cesarino, have escaped to the castle, and with them Renzo and Oratio Baleono. No one was spared by the plunderers.

Desire their ambassador to beg the king and Wolsey for the aid they have long promised, lest the enemy gain everything, and make the emperor monarch of the world. Will do all they can, but the king knows that their strength is not sufficient to restrain the enemy. Florence has entered their League, and will supply 250 men-at-arms, 500 light horse and 5,000 foot till the end of the war, with all necessaries. (Venice, 12 May 1527)

Clerk to Wolsey

News has come that the duke of Bourbon was slain in an attack on Rome on the 6th, and that the pope and cardinals had taken refuge in Sant'Angelo. 45,000 have been slain without regard to age or sex; many friars and priests murdered. The Venetians have promised assistance, but I think it will take no effect. The king of France has sent to raise 10,000 Swiss, and says he is hourly expecting news from De Tarbes. It is said that the Imperialists propose that the pope should surrender Castle Angelo, pay 300,000 ducats, go into Spain and submit to the emperor. Francis is willing to accept the two gentlemen recommended by the king, but I think they will not easily be admitted into the chamber. I think Dr Stephen Gardiner's oration very eloquent. I shall keep myself to generalities. No tale is liked here so well as a short one. (Paris, 28 May 1527)

Treaty between Francis I and Henry VIII

For the entertainment of an army of 30,000 foot and 1,000 lance-knights in Italy against the enemy. Sir Thomas More and Stephen Gardiner, archdeacon of Taunton, acting as commissioners for England, and Gabriel de Grammont, bishop of Tarbes, and John Joachim, for France. Wolsey's visit to France is here arranged. (Westminster, 29 May 1527)

Bishop of Rochester to Wolsey

On consulting those dumb masters, such authorities as he had at hand, finds that they differ greatly among themselves, some declaring that the thing is prohibited by divine law, others that it is lawful. On mature consideration, thinks he sees an answer to the arguments of those who deny its lawfulness, but not to those of the other side. Cannot see any sound reason to show that it is prohibited by divine law for a brother to marry the wife of a brother

who has died without children; and, considering the fullness of authority given by our Lord to the pope, who can
deny that the latter may give dispensation to that effect, for
any serious cause? But, even admitting the arguments to be
balanced on either side, Fisher would be decided by this:
that it belongs to the pope to clear ambiguous passages of
Scripture, after hearing the opinions of the best divines;
otherwise it is in vain that Christ has said, *Quiequid solveris
in terra erit solutum in coelis, &c.* As the pope, therefore, has
more than once by his act declared that it is lawful to dispense in this case, Fisher thinks this alone should
determine the question. Has, accordingly, no hesitation in
declaring that the dispensation is within the pope's power.
Rochester.

Lee to Henry VIII

Wrote on the 24th May that he had sent one to Bayonne
with a safe-conduct for Poynes and the bishop of Tarbes,
but can hear nothing of them. Has heard of the League of
Italy, and the determination of the king to send 10,000
men against the emperor, and that the cardinal should go
over to arrange a marriage between the princess and the
French king or the dauphin; that you are sending to the
emperor security for 2,000,000 and the restitution of
Sforza. Refers him to his letter to the cardinal. The
emperor is much abashed, and Inigo condemned for being
so scrupulous. I have said I do not believe it, and that you
would not break with the emperor except with great
cause. The emperor is sorry for Bourbon's enterprise
against Rome.

This day the prince was baptised with much pomp.
His name is Philip. His godfathers are the Constable and
the duke of Alba; his godmother the queen of Portugal.
The emperor told nuncio that Bourbon had no commission to act as he had done. Though it may be expedient to

have a general council, it is not expedient to have it at Spires by order of Pompey Colonna. (Valladolid, 5 June 1527)

Cardinal Farnese to Wolsey

Writes by Casale. In their present great calamity, and the nefarious crimes committed against God, the Church and Italy, they look to Wolsey. There is no service which will meet a more divine reward than his help on the present occasion. Will not cease to pray to God for Wolsey's safety; and in regard to the pope and the consistory will use his efforts to advance whatever can tend to the perpetual renown and happiness of the king. (Castle of Sant'Angelo, 6 June 1527)

Campeggio to Wolsey

Writes by Casale, who had been with them at the siege of Sant'Angelo a month complete and has rendered good service. Campeggio has been plundered of all he had, and is compelled to redeem his life with a large sum of money. Wishes his collector in England to gather his rents, and transmit them as soon as possible. (Sant'Angelo, 7 June 1527)

Cardinal Triulzi to Wolsey

The danger of the pope and the Holy See must now be known to Wolsey through Casale, who has been conspicuous in behalf of the afflicted cardinals. They trust to Wolsey for relief, who shares their dignity. (Rome, 8 June, 1527)

Italy

Letters from the prothonotary Casale.

Letters have come from the army, of the 2nd inst., stating that they have determined to go to Viterbo on account of their want of victuals, and it was understood that the pope was treating for a most disgraceful concord. Owing to the fault of the forces of the League, the pope is compelled to give himself up at the discretion of the enemy, to his own destruction. The Imperialists demand 400,000 ducats, and the pope and all the cardinals are in their power. Some are of opinion that the viceroy will treat the pope badly. Thinks, himself, that he will dissemble till he has extorted all the money. Wishes the allied forces had not promised to come to the pope's assistance, for then we should not have suffered so many ills, nor would the pope have been removed from Rome. As his Holiness's expectations are quite destroyed, the Imperialists will be able to go where they like. Hopes they will first go to the duchy of Urbino, and punish the duke as he deserves for having destroyed the pope and Italy. The duke of Ferrara went to Modena, but the city refused to change.

Unless the French king undertakes all that necessity, expediency and honour compel him to perform, everything will go wrong. "These men" are so unjust that they tax even the secretaries and agents of the emperor.

The viceroy went to Rome, and had an interview with the pope in the castle, but what was done is not known. The prince of Orange was very ill from a gunshot wound.

Letters have been sent from Sienna to Ferrara, saying that the pope has agreed to certain conditions, especially to pay 300,000 ducats, and is going to Naples with his court. The report is not believed, however. (In the hand of Vannes. 9 June 1527)

Narrative of Viscount Lisle

Describes minutely a "festyn" which took place on Thursday night in the same hall where "our oration" was made at the palace, the roof and sides of which were covered with rich hangings and "rolls of green box with garlands of the same; and in the garlands were either the arms of England and France, or else visages of antyks". When the king and we were come to the high dais, the young lords and gentlemen began to dance till night came. "And then the kyng weshyd alone, and sait down; and the qween of Navarre weshyd togedyr". The viscount of Toreyn carved before the king; M de Guise, of Lorraine, before the king of Navarre and my lady Renée; and M de Guise de Gee, drink After supper they began to dance again, and the king went in maskyr with Mr Brown and many of the young lords, and danced. There were four kinds of masks: two with long gowns and hoods, and great plumes on the head of divers colours; and one of coats of white satin with laces and cuts. Two were after the Turkish fashion. "And then was a play of shepherds which brought in the Ruin of Rome. After was a proper device of two angels brought in half skochyns, with a joiner's plane in each of their hands, which in French is called *vng peeffe*, and over planed those half skochyns, so that they made them one whole skochyn, which awhole was half white, half red. And besides that, the one of those angels had a long branch of a rose in his hand; and written in his breast, in great letters, *Angleterre*, and the other, *France*. And so lovingly holding, they both this hoole skochyn joining made their reverence and departed." The maskers then danced again till two in the morning. I then took my leave of the king and my Lady, and of the queen of Navarre, and returned to my lodging. (In the hand of Lisle)

Wolsey to Henry VIII

Sends by Peter Vannes letters he has received of news from Italy. The king will perceive by them the accursed cruelty of the Imperialists, and their detestable sacrilege. The pope and the cardinals will run all extremities rather than submit. Hopes they will be succoured. (Hampton Court, Trinity Sunday, 16 June 1527)

Wolsey to Ghinucci, Lee and Poyntz

Gives an account of the cruelties committed by the Imperialists at Rome. It is expedient to know whether the emperor justifies the same. They are to remonstrate with him. If he disowns these acts, they are to require him to show some demonstration to that effect and punish his army. If, on the other hand, he is contented with what is done, they are to send word immediately, as it will then be ground for war.

Henry VIII

Commission to Cardinal Wolsey, appointing him his plenipotentiary for concluding a league between Henry, the Emperor, Francis I and the Venetians. (Signed and sealed. London, 18 June 1527)

Commission appointing Cardinal Wolsey as the king's lieutenant and plenipotentiary in France, consequent on the captivity of Clement VII. (London, 18 June 1527)

Commission to Wolsey, ambassador in France, to treat for the projected marriage of Mary with one of the French princes. (London, 18 June 1527)

Commission for an offensive league against the emperor. (London, 20 June 1527)

A memorial of things to be treated of by Wolsey with the French king:

1 That, if the French king will agree to it, "the determination of the alternative for the marriage of my lady princess be in the person of the duke of Orleans"; the dowry and securities requisite to be committed to Wolsey's discretion.

2 If Francis will not consent, "the said alternative to be

resolved *in neutrum*", with the provisions mentioned in the treaty *arctioris conjunctionis*.

3   "To amplify and extend the peace perpetual", and convert the provision for carrying on war in Flanders, according to the defensive league, into a contribution for the defence of Italy.

4   To arrange the order of the personal meeting; the place to be at Calais.

5   To conclude a league with the pope, France and the Venetians, for defence of Italy, "and re-integration of the state of the pope's Holiness and the Church into the pristine manner", with a pension to the king of 30,000 ducats.

6   To treat for universal or particular peace between all Christian princes.

7   To declare the utmost that the king will consent to have offered to the emperor for redemption of the French king's children, and payment of the king's debts.

8   To take measures with the French king to prevent the indiction of a General Council at the emperor's dictation, the deprivation of the pope, or the translation of the Holy See to Spain or Germany.

9   As Wolsey knows the king's mind upon the premises, and it is impossible to give circumstantial instructions about everything, they are left to his discretion.

(In the hand of Gardiner. Signed at the beginning and end by the king.)

Wolsey to Henry VIII

Is not a little troubled at the message sent from the king by Master Wolman, as if Wolsey questioned the king's secret matter. There is nothing he is so desirous to advance, "not doubting for anything that I have heard so

ever this overture hath come to the queen's knowledge …
than I have done before; and, as I said unto Master
Sampson, if your brother had never known her, by reason
whereof there was no affinity contracted, yet in that she
was married *in facie Ecclesiae,* and contracted *per verba de
praesenti*, there did arise *impedimentum public; honestatis*,
which is no less *impedimentum ad dirimendum matrimonium*
than affinity, whereof the bull maketh no express mention". These are the words Wolsey uttered to Sampson
when he said that the queen was very obstinate, "affirming
that your brother did never know her carnally", and that
she desired to have counsel as well of strangers as of
English—a device which never could have come into her
head except it had been suggested; and therefore Wolsey
suggested that the king should handle her gently, until it
was shown what the pope and Francis would do. Norfolk
and Suffolk were present on the occasion. Begs the king
will believe that in all things concerning the king's honour
Wolsey will be constant, even if all others should fail. (In
the hand of Gardiner. Westminster, 1 July 1527)

Henry VIII to Anne Boleyn

I have been in great agony about the contents of your letters, not knowing whether to construe them to my
disadvantage *comme en des aucunes autres*, or to my advantage. I beg to know expressly your intention touching the
love between us. Necessity compels me to obtain this
answer, having been more than a year wounded by the dart
of love, and not yet sure whether I shall fail or find a place
in your affection. This has prevented me naming you my
mistress; for if you love me with no more than ordinary
love, the name is not appropriate to you, for it denotes a
singularity far from the common. But if it please you to do
the office of a true, loyal mistress, and give yourself, body
and heart, to me, who have been and mean to be your loyal

servant, I promise you not only the name, but that I shall make you my sole mistress, remove all others from my affection and serve you only. Give me a full answer on which I can rely; and if you do not like to answer by letter, appoint some place where I can have it by word of mouth.

Henry VIII to Anne Boleyn

Though it is not for a gentleman to take his lady in the place of a servant, nevertheless, according to your desire, I shall willingly grant it if thereby I may find you less ungrateful in the place chosen by yourself than you have been in the place given you by me; thanking you most heartily that you are pleased still to have some remembrance of me. 6. N. R. 1. De R. O. M.V. C. Z

Henry VIII to Anne Boleyn

Although, my mistress, you have not been pleased to remember your promise when I was last with you, to let me hear news of you, and have an answer to my last, I think it the part of a true servant to inquire after his mistress's health, and send you this, desiring to hear of your prosperity. I also send by the bearer a buck killed by me late last night, hoping when you eat of it you will think of the hunger. Written by the hand of your servant, who often wishes you in the place of your brother.

Henry VIII to Anne Boleyn

I and my heart put ourselves in your hands. Let not absence lessen your affection; for it causes us more pain than I should ever have thought, reminding us of a point of astronomy that the longer the days are, the further off is the sun, and yet the best is all the greater. So it is with our love, which keeps its fervour in absence, at least on our side. Prolonged absence would be intolerable, but for my firm hope in your indissoluble affection. As I cannot be with you in person, I send you my picture set in bracelets.

Cardinal — to Wolsey

Is not able to come to Wolsey to tell him of the present disaster, and therefore writes to implore his help. They are let in triumph, and deprived of everything—their country, their dignity, their honours. Wishes they had adhered to Wolsey's advice. He remains free, and, being old and infirm, begs Wolsey to protect them. Those on whom hitherto everything depended are prevented by their guards from writing. The court, Rome, Italy, the whole world look to Wolsey, and in this the king will help him. Begs him to use his influence with the emperor. Praises Gregory Casale, who is returning to England. (Venice, 3 July 1527)

Wolsey to Henry VIII

Advertises the king of what occurred since taking his journey from Westminster on Wednesday last. Was everywhere well received by the people of London. Hears also from the archbishop of Canterbury and Sir Edward Gildeford, who resorted unto him, that the realm was never in better quiet, in spite of all report to the contrary. Lodged on the first night of his journey at Sir John Wilteshere's, and was met by the archbishop, with whom he communicated on the king's secret matter; what had been done in it; how displeasantly the queen takes it; what the king has done to pacify her; declaring that hitherto nothing had been intended by the king, except to discover the truth, on occasion moved by the bishop of Tarbes. Watched his countenance, and observed his astonishment how the queen should come to the knowledge of it. Thinks he is not much turned from his first fashion, as he asserts that, however displeasant it may be to the queen, truth and the law must prevail. I have instructed him how he is to act if the queen should ask his counsel, and he has promised to comply. Spoke to him of the present calamities of the Church, the captivity of the pope, and your resolutions for redress of the same, for which purpose I was sent to France.

Proceeded next to Rochester, where I arrived on Thursday and was received by Sir Edward and Sir Henry Gildeford, and entertained by the bishop, to whom I talked of the lamentable state of the Church and the prayers and fastings ordered by you for redress of the same. On my asking whether any one had been sent to him from the queen, he paused awhile, and in conclusion said that he had received a message from the queen by word of mouth, without any particulars, stating that certain matters had happened between her and you, in which she desired his counsel; that he had replied that in such matters he would do nothing without the king's commandment. On my asking him to be plain and frank with me, and tell me if he had formed any conjecture what the matter could be, he answered that he knew nothing certain, but conjectured it was for a divorce, and he was induced so to think by a tale brought by his brother from London, who had heard in certain company things sounded to such a purpose. This is all he says. I then told him that the king had never intended to disclose this matter, except to very few; yet now, seeing that his good intentions had been misrepresented, I had special commission to inform him of it, taking from him an oath of secrecy. I then told him the whole matter of the proposed marriage between Francis and the Princess Mary, and the objection made by the bishop of Tarbes, and the investigations to which it had given rise, as to the dispensing powers of the pope, etc., for which I was sent into France; thus declaring the whole matter unto him as was devised with you at York Place. I added that some inkling of the matter had come to the queen's knowledge, who, casting further doubts than was intended, had "broken with your Grace thereof after a very displeasant manner, saying that by my procurement and setting forth a divorce was purposed between her and your Highness", and your anxiety to discover who was her informant. The bishop greatly blamed the conduct of the queen, and thought if he might speak with her he might bring her to submission. I have, however, so persuaded him that he shall not speak or do anything in this matter, except according to your pleasure. After this I had some conversation with him, urging the impediments of the marriage, in which he mainly agreed.

Between Sitenborne and Faversham I encountered the ambassador (Jerome à Lasco) from the vaivode, calling himself king of Hungary, imploring your aid against the Turk. He protested that his master was not seeking an alliance with the Turk, and that he had been promised assistance from the French king. The king may well refuse aid, and avoid the displeasure of Ferdinand, on the ground that he must look to the Church. The ambassador had thought of proposing an alliance with Madame Renée, but on seeing her had devised for a marriage with Madame Eleanor, sister of the emperor. Urged the dishonour of adhering to the Turk. He told me there was much disorder in the French king's council, who was destitute of good captains and money and is in a perplexing and melancholy plight. (In the hand of Gardiner. Faversham, 5 July 1527)

Bishop Fisher to Paul

[Paul says he has heard two things from Doncaster, at which he marvels not a little: 1. that Wakefield has found something in Hebrew which makes for the king's argument; and 2. that the bishops who at first dissented have all come over to the king's opinion; which, if true, he thinks a great disgrace.]

Thanks him for this candid expression of opinion. The matter concerns not only the honour but the soul's health of the writer, if he were to recant what he had once said truly. Trusts he will never depart from the truth, though open to conviction. Has taken great pains in this matter to know what the truth is, and has no doubt of his conclusion. Gives his reasons for holding, in opposition to Wakefield, that marriage with a deceased brother's wife was not prohibited by the Mosaic law. Believes the king means to do nothing against the law of God, but he will be quite justified in submitting his difficulties to the pope; especially as kings, from the fullness of their power, are apt to think that right which suits their pleasure. But it is not true that *all* the bishops think such a marriage invalid.

Rich. Pace to Henry VIII

Sent a letter to the king yesterday, and a book written by the counsel of Master Wakefeld. Answers the objection of some of the king's counsel, that *Leviticus* is annulled by *Deuteronomy*. Wakefeld desires to know whether the king is willing to hear the truth in this great matter. He offers to "show unto your highness such things as no man within your realm can attain unto or show the like, and as well for you as against you". But he does not meddle in this matter without your licence. Pace commends him for his excellent learning and wonderful knowledge. Sends a Hebrew alphabet, desiring it may be delivered to Master Fox with order to get it by heart; by so doing he shall in one month be able to judge of the correctness of the Vulgate and the LXX, and to show the king the truth. (Syon House, Friday)

R. Wakefield to Henry VIII

Offers to defend the king's cause in all the universities of Christendom. Begs the king will keep it secret from man or woman until he hears from Pace. "If the people should know that I, which began to defend the queen's cause, not knowing that she was carnally known of Prince Arthur your brother, should now write against it, surely I should be stoned of them to death, or else have such a slander and obloquy raised upon me, that I had rather to die a thousand times or suffer it. I have and will in such manner answer to the bishop of Rochester's book that I trust he shall be ashamed to wade or meddle any further in the matter." Has shown part of his book to Pace. (Syon House, London)

Rich. Pace to John Pace

To my loving brother John Pace. Whatsoever is spoken here of my lord cardinal's evil mind against me, it is untrue, for he hath nothing done against me but that is to my high contentation, and rather advancement than hindrance. And thus I heartily pray you and command you to show to all my friends, and to publish the same abroad. I wrote to his grace this day to admit you to his service. Let me have knowledge what he will say thereunto. (From Syon, this Friday)

Pace to his brother John Pace

Sir, I command you, immediately upon the sight hereof, to repair to me hither, with all my servants, as many as will come; and bring with you also your wife and children, one maid to wait upon her, leaving the other to keep your house. And do you set written upon the door "God save the king. Amen." I know the king's mind. Do you as I command you, whatsoever any other man shall say. (10 July 1527)

Henry VIII to Cardinal Cibo

No one can receive the news of the disaster at Rome, without grief and indignation. What could be more nefarious among Christians than to conspire the destruction of that city, and to treat with contumely the Vicar of Christ. They have not even spared holy places, but have imprisoned the pope, and committed all kinds of sacrilege. As a champion of the Faith, is determined to resist this storm, and leave nothing undone to restore the pope to liberty and vindicate the dignity of the Church. Has no doubt the cardinal, and those of his brethren who have been spared this degrading bondage, burn with the same zeal. Has accordingly despatched the cardinal of York to the French king, to consult upon this matter. Hopes Cibo will meet him, and take measures for the pope's liberation. "Ex Regia (nostra Windsor)" (10 July 1527)

Wolsey to Henry VIII

This day, according to his letter by Basing, embarked between 3 and 4 o'clock in the morning, and arrived at Calais by 9. Had a long discourse with the deputy and others at Calais. Finds these errors he will amend at his return. Found news here from the prothonotary Casale, dated Venice, 14th June, which he has translated out of Italian into Latin. Intends to write tomorrow to the English ambassadors with the French king. (In the hand of Gardiner. Calais, 11 July)

Ludovicus Vives to Henry VIII

Knowing that the king, however much he is engrossed by the affairs of all Europe, always finds time for study, sends him a copy of an epitome of the *Adagia* of Erasmus, which, as he told him, he had been unable to procure in London. Has prepared an answer to Luther's letter, which he is ready to publish with the king's annotations when he received them, or to send to be printed at London. Hears that Wolsey is going to France, and that he will settle the affairs of Christendom. (Bruges, 13 July 1527)

MID-JULY 1527 TO SEPTEMBER 1527

Wolsey has tried to settle the matter of the divorce before Katherine realised what was happening. However, with great difficulty, she appealed first to her nephew, Charles, in the hope of preserving her marriage and the inheritance of her daughter Mary. To Katherine, in the Catholic faith, divorce would be a mortal sin.

Knight to Wolsey

On the 10th received your packet, with a letter for the king's highness, which I delivered at the More. Received another packet on the 14th, with a letter for the king, which I delivered at Enfield. De Lasko, the Hungarian ambassador, delivered his charge this day, dilating on the miserable state of Hungary and the free election of the vaivode. The king ordered the dean of his chapel (Sampson) to reply. Gives the substance of the speech. The ambassador had his brother Stanyslaus with him. The king ordered me to send this account to you.

Fraunçoise Philippe, the Spaniard, sewer to the Queen, has laboured to obtain licence to go into Spain to visit his mother, who is sick. The queen has refused her assent, and laboured with the king to prevent it, but the king, knowing great collusion and dissimulation between them, doth also dissemble; feigning that Philippe's desire is made upon ground and consideration, and easily hath persuaded the queen to be content with his going. And because it was thought dangerous for him to pass through France, or, at this season, by the seas, the king hath said, that in case Philippe be taken by enemies his highness will redeem him, and pay his ransom; and this policy the king useth to bring Philippe in more firm confidence; but his pleasure is, and also he desireth and prayeth your grace to use such policy as, notwithstanding any safe-conduct that the said Philippe shall obtain, either by your grace's means, or any other, of the French king, he may be let, impeached and detained in some quarter of France, so that it be not in anywise known that the said let, arrest or deprehension should come by the king, by your grace or any of the king's subjects. The king's highness doth perceive that the queen is the only cause of the man's going into Spain, as he that is and hath been always privy unto the queen's affairs and secrets. The king desires Wolsey to send word to the bishop of Worcester to keep a look-out for such as resort to the emperor's court. (Enfield, 15 July 1527)

Clement VII

Bull referring to the pope's personal danger from the plague during his imprisonment, some of the officers of his chamber having died of it; and empowering the cardinals, in the event of his death taking place while in captivity, to meet in Bologna, Perugia or Ancona for the election of the future pope; or, if these cities be under interdict, or in open rebellion against the Church, in Florence, Turin or Mantua. The election to take place wherever a majority of the cardinals agree that it shall be held. But if the See fall vacant when the pope is away from Italy, the election is to take place at Rome, unless that city be in rebellion. In the first case absent cardinals are to be waited for 10 days; in the second, a month. Castle of Sant'Angelo, Rome, 1527, id. Julii; 4 Clement VII.

In the hand of Cardinal Armellinus, who also adds the following mandate of the pope to Cardinal Armellinus, his chamberlain, to sign and seal the printed copies of this bull in token of its authenticity. (Signed and sealed. 18 July 1527)

Knight to Wolsey

Received today two packets from him for the king, who, after reading them, summoned his council, and bade Knight read to them clerk's letters, the copies of Sanga's *nuncii apostolici ad nuncium in anglia*, and those of John Joachim. He was glad that the Florentines had joined the Italian League, that Lautrec is advancing so diligently, and that so many Swiss have descended. After saying that he hoped soon to hear of some notable act against the Imperialists, he ordered Knight to write to Wolsey, desiring him to advance as speedily as possible towards the French king, to Paris if need be, and conclude with him before an answer returned by the ambassador lately sent to the emperor. Has told him that the king had given a passport to Fraunçoise Philippe, the Queen's sewer; but finding that the cause of his going was feigned for certain purposes of the queen, he wishes him secretly to be stopped and molested in some part of France, that he may not reach Spain. If he does not pass by Wolsey, he wishes notice to be sent to my lord of Worcester, that he may discover what charge he has. This is a matter the king esteems highly. (Howndysdowne, 18 July 1527)

Wolsey to Henry VIII

Thanks the king for the news contained in Knight's letter of the 15th. The king is right in thinking that the purpose of Philippe in going to Spain is to disclose the 'secret matter'' unto the emperor, and devise means for preventing it. Should it come to the emperor's ears it will prove no little hindrance. If he comes this way, Wolsey will have him stopped; if he goes by sea to Spain, nothing can prevent him. The best means, therefore, will be for the king to prevent him from going to Spain by sea. (In the hand of Gardiner. Calais, 19 July 1527)

Ghinucci, Lee and Poyntz to Wolsey

The emperor sent Buclans to me [Lee] after the dispatch of my servant, desiring that someone might be sent after him. He wished Lee to inform Wolsey, who, he hears, has arrived in France, that he had just received letters from his ambassador there, stating that a great personage had asked him to write to the emperor to come to terms:

> [In cipher] That Francis had entered league with England, which Wolsey had come to confirm, but as the treaty was injurious to Francis he was putting off meeting with him till he heard from De Tarbes, as he would fain do somewhat with the emperor first. He said Wolsey might be assured he would not be swayed by their craft to do anything without the consent of England.

(Valladolid, 22 July 1527)

Ghinucci to Wolsey

It is the object of the Imperialists to bring over to their views the king of England, or at all events to separate him from France, and therefore they have no thoughts of peace, whatever they pretend, or whatever conditions be offered them. They think the union between France and England will not last. The French seem to be very anxious for peace, and in all conferences with the Imperialists that some handle should be given by which they or we might renew the colloquy with them. They urge us to do this as of ourselves, showing that they are anxious for a treaty of peace; on which account they offered by Avemaria 3,000,000. The emperor told us that he had little trust in it until the bishop of Tarbes, wishing to clear his master of it, did, in fact, prove it. For, finding the friar in his house, he bade him tell us what instructions he had received; and he, beginning at the close and not at the commencement of his commission, said that Lautrec at the friar's departure had ordered him not to spare money for the liberation of the French king's children; that he had offered 1,000,000. I know well that never less than 1,000,000 was offered, and I suspect that it was increased by a million. I guess as much from the emperor's hint, and that it was proposed to pay by instalments. Doubtless Wolsey knows the certainty of the matter. Good authorities think that the envoy sent by the emperor has no commission to liberate the pope, and what is given out here is done only to stop people's mouths. It is rumoured that your reverence is going into France to separate the Church of England and of France from the Roman, not merely during the captivity of the pope and to effect his liberation, but for a perpetual division.

Francis I

Commission of Francis I, empowering Cardinal Wolsey to pardon and set at liberty, in the towns that he passes by, such prisoners as he shall please, under his own letters patent, except in cases of treason, murder, rape, forgery and similar crimes. (St Denis, July 1527)

Wolsey to Henry VIII

Received letters from the ambassadors in Spain, with a schedule of the emperor's demands. Sends copies with marginal comments. Although the demands are very high, beyond what the king deemed convenient, thinks that, as he is willing to modify them at Henry's request, some good may ensue, and is not sorry that they bear "a visage of some difficulty" until the cardinal has concluded what he has to do with the French king. From what he has seen is in hope that the king's matter shall pass with Francis, for which he has made the best speed he could; but Francis desired to meet him at Amiens, where he cannot be before Thursday, in consequence of his mother's illness. Points out the dangers likely to ensue from the intentions of the emperor to draw the pope into Spain. To prevent this he has urged the French king to set forth his fleet under Andrea Doria, and purposes to write to the pope pointing out the dangers that are likely to ensue.

Has had a long talk with Gregory Casale of the lamentable affairs at Rome, and thinks that the pope's letter to the king, written with his own hand, will stir up his zeal in the Church's cause. Has received by Casale similar letters of the pope and of the cardinals in captivity, and is so moved with sorrow that he is ready to shed his life and blood in their behalf. Commends Casale for his conduct, and intends to make him commissary of the foot to be sent to Italy. Has practised with the marquis of Mantua "to come into the parties of the League". Thinks the Venetian ambassador should be spoken to, that the *Signory* may be made more diligent. Is extremely well entertained, but finds in all the towns great dearth, misery and poverty, and very ill lodging, very inferior to those in England. Sends a decipher of the bishop of Worcester's letters, by which the king will see that the emperor wishes to sow suspicion between France and England. (In the hand of Gardiner. Abbeville, 29 July 1527)

Wolsey to Henry VIII

Daily and hourly musing, and thinking on your grace's great and secret affair, and how the same may come to good effect and desired end, as well for the deliverance of your grace out of the thrauld, pensive and dolorous life that the same is in, as for the continuance of your health, etc. I consider that the pope's consent must be gained in case the queen should decline my jurisdiction, or the approbation of the cardinals be had. For the first the pope's deliverance will be necessary, for the other the convocation of the cardinals in France. The pope's deliverance cannot be accomplished except by a peace between the emperor and the French king, which is not likely, considering the high demands of the former; but I will endeavour to see what can be done in this matter. If the pope were delivered, I doubt not he would be easily induced to do everything to your satisfaction.

The cardinals can meet at no place except at Avignon, whither I propose to repair to devise with them for the government of the Church during the pope's captivity, which shall be a good ground and fundament for the effectual execution of your grace's secret affair. As I shall then be within 100 miles of Perpignan—a commodious place to treat with the emperor—I think it would be desirable that a meeting should be held between him, the French king's mother and me; and in the event of the emperor persisting in unreasonable demands, I, and the rest of the cardinals in France, may then make declaration that we will not be bound by anything the pope may do in his captivity. Though I have devised this for the advancement of your particular affair, being ready and prone to do all things that may confer thereunto, it is not my intention that this meeting with the emperor shall take place unless I am constrained to go to Avignon. (In the hand of Gardiner. Abbeville, 29 July 1527)

Henry VIII to Anne Boleyn

For a present so beautiful that nothing could be more so I thank you most heartily, not only for the splendid diamond and the ship in which the solitary damsel is tossed about, but also for the pretty interpretation and too humble submission made by your benignity. I should have found it difficult to merit this but for your humanity and favour, which I have sought and will seek to preserve by every kindness possible to me; and this is my firm intention and hope, according to the motto, *Aut illic aut nullibi.* Your letter, and the demonstrations of your affection, are so cordial that they bind me to honour, love and serve you. I desire also, if at any time I have offended you, that you will give me the same absolution that you ask, assuring you that henceforth my heart shall be devoted to you only. I wish my body also could be. God can do it if he pleases, to whom I pray once a day that it may be, and hope at length to be heard. Escripte de la main du secretaire qui en coeur, corps et volonté est vostre loaill et plus assuré serviteure,

H. aultre (Coeur) ne cherse R.

Henry VIII to Anne Boleyn

The time seems so long since I heard of your good health and of you, that I send the bearer to be better ascertained of your health and your purpose; for since my last parting from you I have been told you have quite given up the intention of coming to court, either with your mother or otherwise. If so, I cannot wonder sufficiently; for I have committed no offence against you, and it is very little return for the great love I bear you to deny me the presence of the woman I esteem most of all the world. If you love me as I hope you do, our separation should be painful to you. I trust your absence is not wilful on your part; for if so, I can but lament my ill fortune, and by degrees abate my great folly.

Wolsey to Ghinucci and Lee

Compliments them on their circumspection, of which the king and he have so high an opinion that he is ordered to entrust them with the most secret matters. A rumour, somehow or another, has sprung up in England that proceedings are being taken for a divorce between the king and queen, which is entirely without foundation, yet not altogether causeless; for there has been some discussion about the papal dispensation, not with any view to a divorce, but to satisfy the French, who have raised the objection on proposing a marriage between the princess and their sovereign. The proceedings which took place on this dispute gave rise to the rumour, and reached the ears of the queen, who expressed some resentment, but was satisfied after explanation; and no suspicion exists, except perchance the queen may have communicated with the emperor on the subject. You are to discover if anything of this kind has taken place; for, from the time the rumour began, Ferdinand her physician left, and afterwards Fraunçoise Philippe. As the whole rumour is false, I should be sorry if the emperor believed it, lest these lies should prove an obstacle to the peace.

You are to watch Ferdinand and Francis; and, if the emperor drops a word of the subject, make such a prudent reply as will overcome his prejudices. You are to say nothing about the French objections. But, if you hear anything started, answer summarily that no dissolution of the marriage is intended, but only the confirmation of it, in the event of any question being raised, and that it is foolish to suppose so grave a cause could be decided in private. I have told you all the circumstances, by which you will gather how unfounded the rumour is. You will observe silence with regard to the objections of the French. The bishop of Worcester is to return. (Abbeville, 1 August 1527)

Wolsey to Henry VIII

Though I have found much affection in the French king, I have forborne at present to speak of your private matter, deferring the same till I have put your affairs in perfect train. I hope he will agree, and for this I study the means day and night. I have received letters from Hacket, out of Flanders, stating that it has come to my Lady Margaret's knowledge that you intend to be divorced. No doubt, therefore, the emperor has knowledge of it, and will do all he can at Rome to prevent it. I have therefore, by the advice of my lord of Bath, devised certain expeditions to be made to Rome, as well by the bishop of Worcester, for whom I have sent with all diligence to come hither, as by Gregory Casale and the pope's ambassador (Salviati). And I have not spared money in order to get access to the pope to obtain his consent for convoking the cardinals during his captivity, etc.

As I have found the French king so compliant it will not be necessary for me to go to Spain; and the same would be dangerous, as you have advertised me. As it is your request I should send Master Stephen Gardiner to receive your instructions, I beg you will forbear the same till he shall be advertised of such expedition as I have, and shall conceive for the advancement of your secret matter, as he is the only instrument I have for the purpose. If I should send him he will be in peril of his life, for both he and I are much weakened by the excessive heat and continual labour. I will send Dr Alen to learn your pleasure. (In the hand of Gardiner. Amiens, 11 August 1527)

Erasmus to Stephen Gardiner

Was pleased to have his recollection refreshed by Gardiner's letters, but did not require such minute indications. The image of you which I saw at Paris still remains fresh in my mind. I recognise the same intellectual dexterity in letters and in graver business as you showed at Paris in domestic management (*in œconomucus*). Your letters were not more agreeable to me than were the salads dressed by your art agreeable to my palate. I am glad to find we have one and the same patron (Wolsey), and that you stand so well with him. Begs his compliments to Francis the physician, Toneys, Burbank and Peter ab Arenis (Vannes). (Basle, 3 September 1527)

Wolsey to Henry VIII

Although, by letters to the bishop of Bath, your majesty has been advertised of the news, yet, as I am informed by Knight's letter of the 29th, and by the bishop of Bath's letter of the 30th, that you intend to send him to Rome to promote your secret matter, and other things, I think it necessary to say:

1   That the French will not proceed to the renunciation of Milan, or aid the emperor to obtain the Crown Imperial, except in a qualified manner.
2   I am fully assured by the bishop of Worcester that the emperor has no intention of giving the duchy of Milan to the duke of Richmond, and the offer was only intended to deceive the king.
3   I am assured, on oath, that the bishop of Tarbes had no

secret instructions in negotiating with Lady Eleanor, beyond what is known to the English ambassadors, and that his purpose in going is to procure more easy terms from the emperor through her intervention, which I think not undesirable.

4   I am afraid the cardinals will not be persuaded to come to Avignon, especially as they have been commanded by the pope not to leave Italy. I purpose, however, to devise articles for the government of the Church, with the papal legate Salviati, and other French cardinals, in case the emperor will not deliver the pope.

5   I am of opinion that the bishop of Worcester will be a more suitable negotiator with the pope than the secretary (Knight), as he has more experience and will have easier access to his Holiness, for which he has letters from the emperor. My lord of Worcester is privy to your secret matter, and will more readily obtain a general faculty for me by which, without informing the pope of your purpose, I may delegate such judges as the queen will not refuse; and if she does, the cognisance of the cause shall be devolved upon me, and by a clause to be inserted in the general commission no appeal be allowed from my decision to the pope; and also I may obtain protestation as contained in the minutes sent to the bishop of Bath. These two commissions may also be entrusted to the nuncio Gambara, that he may negotiate with the pope, in the event of the bishop of Worcester being refused admission. I am the more bent upon this, as I hear the pope has been sent to Gaieta under strict guard. I have instructed Gregory (Casale), after he has settled with Lautrec and Sir Robt Jerningham, to gain access to the pope; and between this and Saturday I will despatch Worcester and Gambara.

Since the bishop of Bath left, I have had long conferences with the dean of the rota (Staffileo), who is now
convinced that the pope's dispensation is invalid. He has
written a book in support of his opinion, which I will
bring with me. He is ready to maintain his opinion in
England. "If your grace will take a little patience", and suffer such things to be done as shall be devised for the
purpose, "your intent shall honourably and lawfully take
the desired effect".

News is come that, from dread of Lautrec, the
Spaniards have carried the pope to Gaieta, who was not
sorry to leave Rome, in consequence of the pestilence. The
emperor's army die in great numbers, and his affairs are
ruinous, and will be more so when Andrea Doria arrives
at Naples with the French galleys. Cæsar Fregoso has made
an attack upon Genoa and killed more than 1,000. I am
told by Worcester that the emperor, whatever he may
report, will not relent at any request you may make; but his
drift is, with fair words, to deceive you, and prevent your
stricter union with the French. He also told me that, on
hearing how by the detention of the pope the churches of
England and of France would decline from their obedience, the emperor had sent the general of the Observants
to set the pope at liberty, and induce him to come into
Spain, where he will probably be poisoned, and the See
Apostolic established in Spain for ever. Methods have,
however, been taken to prevent the pope's voyage.
Worcester also told me that before he left Spain the
emperor knew of your intention to be divorced, by the
report of English merchants, and probably of Fraunçoise
Philippe, who has arrived and held communication with
the emperor for a whole day. Let me have the confirmation of the treaty of perpetual peace, which I have
promised to deliver before my departure. It has been
arranged that there shall be a duplicate one sealed with

green wax, the other with gold, to be interchangeably delivered.

P. S. As I was enclosing these letters, the French king sent me the marquis of Saluce's letters, with an account of the Imperialists.

If this letter be not elegantly indited, I beg you will take it in good part, as it was written at night. (Compiègne, 5 September 1527)

Henry VIII to Erasmus

Is grieved to hear from the archbishop of Canterbury that Erasmus thinks he is in danger.

In my tender years, when I first knew you, I entertained for you no slight regard; and this has been daily augmented by the honourable mention you have made of me in your writings. Now, seeing the unwearied labours which you have suffered in the cause of Christianity, I am desirous of succouring your pious efforts, for I have myself felt for some years the same desire of restoring the faith and religion of Christ to its pristine dignity, and repelling the impious attacks of the heretics, that the word of God may run on purely and freely. But such is the infelicity of the times, and the prostration of good manners, that all things degenerate. I am anxious for your safety, lest, if you were removed, heresy should advance with greater danger and greater cruelty. I remember you used to say that England should be your refuge in your old age. I shall consider your conversation and advice as a great advantage; and we will, with united efforts, advance the gospel of Christ. (18 September 1527)

— to the grand marshal of France (Montmorency)

Has been informed by the "said" personage, who is very familiar with the vice-chancellor of Flanders, the cardinal of Liège, and De Berghes, that some persons in England who favour the emperor are intriguing against the king and cardinal because the king is putting away his wife, the emperor's aunt, which, they say, will make it impossible ever to reconcile the emperor to Henry; and if the latter were dead, they could re-marry the queen or her daughter to some prince of England, who would make perpetual alliance with the emperor against King Francis.

FEBRUARY 1528 TO OCTOBER 1528

Under pressure from the emperor, but desiring to please Henry, the pope has decided to delegate the judgement over the divorce to Campeggio and Wolsey, who will preside over a hearing in London. Campeggio is sent as legate with the commission, but also with instructions not to be too much in haste.

Henry VIII to Anne Boleyn

The bearer and his fellow are dispatched with as many things to compass our matter and bring it to pass as wit could imagine; which being accomplished by their diligence, I

trust you and I will shortly have our desired end. This
would be more to my heart's ease and quietness of my
mind than anything in the world. I assure you no time
would be lost, for *ultra posse non est esse*. Keep him not too
long with you, but desire him, for your sake to make the
more speed; for the sooner we shall have word from him,
the sooner shall our matter come to pass. And thus, upon
trust of your short repair to London, I make an end of my
letter; mine own sweetheart. Written with the hand of him
which desireth as much to be yours as you do to have him.
(February 1528)

Anne Boleyn to Wolsey

My lord, in my most humble wise I desire you to pardon
me that I am so bold to trouble you with my simple and
rude writing, proceeding from one who is much desirous
to know that your grace does well, as I perceive by this
bearer. The great pains you take for me, both day and
night, are never likely to be recompensed, but alonely in
loving you, next unto the king's grace, above all creatures
living, as my deeds shall manifest. I long to hear from you
news of the legate, and hope they will be very good.

[Added by the king] The writer of this would not
cease till she had called me likewise to set my hand. Both
of us desire to see you and are glad to hear you have
escaped the plague so well, trusting the fury of it is abated,
especially with those who keep good diet, as I trust you
do. The not hearing of the legate's arrival in France causeth
us somewhat to muse; but we trust by your diligence
shortly to be eased of that trouble. (June 1528)

Henry VIII to Anne Boleyn

There came to me in the night the most afflicting news
possible. I have to grieve for three causes: first, to hear of
my mistress's sickness, whose health I desire as my own,

and would willingly bear the half of yours to cure you; secondly, because I fear to suffer yet longer that absence which has already given me so much pain—God deliver me from such an importunate rebel!; thirdly, because the physician I trust most is at present absent when he could do me the greatest pleasure. However, in his absence, I send you the second, praying God he shall soon make you well, and I shall love him the better, and then I hope to see you soon again. (June 1528)

Henry VIII to Anne Boleyn

The doubt I had of your health troubled me extremely, and I should scarcely have had any quiet without knowing the certainty; but since you have felt nothing, I hope it is with you as with us. When we were at Waltham, two ushers, two valets de chambres, your brother Master Treasurer, fell ill and are now quite well, without one sick person. I think if you would retire from Surrey, as we did, you would avoid all danger. Another thing may comfort you: few women have this illness; and moreover none of our court and few elsewhere have died of it. I beg you, therefore, not to distress yourself at our absence, for whoever strives against fortune is often the furthest from his end. (June 1528)

Henry VIII to Anne Boleyn

The cause of my writing at this time, good sweetheart, is only to understand of your good health and prosperity, whereof to know I would be glad as in manner mine own; praying God that (and it be His pleasure) to send us shortly together, for I promise you I long for it, howbeit trust it shall not be long; and seeing my darling is absent, I can no less do than to send her some flesh representing my name, which is hart's flesh for Henry, prognosticating that hereafter, God willing, you must enjoy some of mine, which, He pleased, I would were now. As touching your sister's matter, I have caused Walter Welshe to write to my lord my mind therein, whereby I trust that Eve shall not have the power to deceive Adam; for surely whatsoever is said, it cannot so stand with his honour but that he must needs take her his natural daughter now in her extreme necessity. No more to you at this time my own darling but that a while I would we were together of an evening. With the hand of yours, etc. (June 1528)

Henry VIII to Anne Boleyn

Since here last, Walter Welshe, Master Browne, Thomas Care, Yrion of Brearton, John Coke, the Pothecary, are fallen of the sweat in this house, and, thank God, all have recovered, so the plague has not quite ceased here. The rest of us are well and, I hope, will pass it. As for the matter of Wylton, my lord cardinal has had the nuns before him and examined them in the presence of Master Bell who assures me that she whom we would have had abbess has confessed herself to have had two children by two different priests and has since been kept, not long ago, by a servant of the Lord Broke that was. Wherefore I would not, for all the gold in the world, cloak your conscience or mine to make her ruler of a house which is of so ungodly demeanour; nor I trust would you that, neither for brother nor sister, I should disdain my honour or conscience. And as touching the prioress or Dame Eleanor's elder sister, though there is not any evident case proved against them, and the prioress is so old that of many years she could not be as she was named, yet notwithstanding, to do you pleasure, I have done that neither of them shall have it, but that some other good and well-disposed woman shall have it, whereby the house shall be better reformed, whereof I assure it hath much need, and God much the better served. As touching your abode at Hever, do therein as best shall like you, for you know best what air doth best with you;

but I would it were come thereto, if it pleased God, that neither of us need care for that, for I ensure you I think it long. Ashby de la Zouche is fallen sick of the sweat, and therefore I send you this bearer, because I think you long to hear tidings from us, as we do in likewise from you. (July 1528)

Anne Boleyn to Wolsey

In most humble wise that my poor heart can think, I thank your grace for your kind letter and rich present, which I shall never be able to deserve without your help; of the which I have so great plenty that all the days of my life I am most bound of all your creatures, next the king's grace, to love and serve your grace. I beseech you never to doubt that I shall ever vary from this thought while breath is in my body. As to your grace's trouble with the sweat, I thank God that those who I desired and prayed for have escaped, namely the king and you. I much desire the coming of the legate, and, if it be God's pleasure, I pray Him to bring this matter shortly to a good end, when I trust partly to recompense your pains. (July 1528)

Henry VIII to Anne Boleyn

The approach of the time which has been delayed so long delights me so much that it seems almost already come. Nevertheless the entire accomplishment cannot be till the two persons meet; which meeting is more desired on my part than anything in the world, for what joy can be so great as to have the company of her who is my most dear friend, knowing likewise that she does the same. Judge then what will that personage do whose absence has given me the greatest pain in my heart, which neither tongue nor writing can express and nothing but that can remedy. Tell your father on my part that I beg him to abridge by two days the time appointed that he may be in court before the old term, or at least upon the day prefixed; otherwise I shall think he will not do the lovers' turn as he said he would, nor answer my expectations. No more for want of time. I hope soon to tell you by mouth the rest of the pains I have suffered in your absence. Written by the hand of the secretary who hopes to be privately with you. (July 1528)

Henry VIII to Anne Boleyn

Is perplexed with such things as her brother will declare to her. Wrote in his last that he trusted shortly to see her "which is better known at London than with any that is about me; whereof I not a little marvel, but lack of discreet handling must be the cause thereof. I hope soon our meeting will not depend on other men's light handylleness but upon your own. Written with the hand of hys who longeth to be yours." (August 1528)

Henry VIII to Anne Boleyn

Writes to tell her of the great elengenes he finds since her departure, "for, I ensure you, me thinketh the time longer since your departing now last than I was wont to do a whole fortnight". Could not have thought so short an absence would have so grieved him, but is comforted now he is coming towards her; "inasmuch as my book maketh substantially for my matter; in token whereof I have spent above four hours this day, which caused me to write a shorter letter to you at this time by cause of some pain in my head. Wishing myself especially an evening in my sweetheart's arms, whose pretty dubbys I trust shortly to cusse." (August 1528)

Henry VIII to Anne Boleyn

Has got her a lodging by my lord cardinal's means such as could not have been found hereabouts for all causes, as the bearer will explain.

Nothing more can be done in our other affairs, nor can all dangers be better provided against, so that I trust it will be hereafter to both our comforts; but I defer particulars, which would be too long to write, and not fit to trust to a messenger, till you repair hither. I trust it will not be long to-fore. I have caused my lord your father to make his provisions with speed. (August 1528)

Henry VIII to Anne Boleyn

The reasonable request of your last letter, with the pleasure that I take to know them true, causeth me to send you now these news. The legate which we most desire arrived at Paris on Sunday or Monday last past, so I trust by the next Monday to hear of his arrival at Calais, and then I trust within a while after to enjoy that which I have so longed for to God's pleasure and our both comfort. No more to you at this present, mine own darling, for lack of time, but that I would you were in mine arms, or I in yours, for I think it is long since I kissed you. Written after the killing of an hart at eleven of the clock, minding with God's grace tomorrow mytely tymely to kill another. By the hand of him, which shortly shall be yours. (September 1528)

Campeggio to Salviati

I have not written since leaving Paris. On Wednesday I reached the suburbs of London and lodged at the house of the duke of Suffolk. I was so prostrated by the gout that I could not travel any further either in a litter or on horseback. I am confined to bed, my agony being greater than usual owing to the journey.

As soon as I am able to stand I shall go to the king. On presenting the pope's letter I will exhort him according to my instructions. This has been arranged by the cardinal of York and myself. Subsequently I will do my utmost to persuade the king to abandon the divorce, though I feel sure it will be in vain. I will do the same with the queen who, I doubt not, will show her repugnance. (17 October 1528)

Campeggio to Salviati

The king visited me privately, and we remained together alone for about four hours, discussing only two things. First, I exhorted him not to attempt this matter, in order to confirm and clear his conscience, to establish the succession of the kingdom and to avoid scandals; and that if he had any scruple, he could have a new dispensation.

In the second place, we disputed whether the prohibition existed in the Divine Law, or whether the pope could grant a dispensation; and if he could, whether the dispensation would be valid. His majesty has so diligently studied this matter that I believe in this case he is a great theologian and jurist. He said most plainly that he wanted nothing else than a declaration whether the marriage is valid or not; he himself always presupposing the invalidity; and I believe that an angel descending from Heaven would be unable to persuade him otherwise.

We then discussed a proposal for persuading the queen to enter some religious house. With this he was extremely pleased, and indeed there are good reasons for it. In all other matters the king is determined to allow her whatever she demands, and especially to settle the succession on her daughter in the event of his having no male heirs by another marriage. It was concluded that I and the cardinal should speak to the queen about this on the day following.

Being conveyed in a boat by the cardinal we went on Saturday 24th to execute this mission. The cardinal and I conversed alone with the queen about two hours. Her majesty replied to us that she knew the sincerity of her own conscience; and that she wished to die in the Holy

Faith and in accordance with the commands of God and the Holy Church and she wished to declare her conscience only to Our Lord, and that for the present she would give no other reply. (25 October 1528)

Campeggio to Salviati

The cardinal told me that the queen had asked permission of the king to come and confess to me; which he had granted her. Accordingly at nine o'clock, the second hour of the day she came privately and was with me for a long space. Although she told me all under the seal of confession, yet also she gave me liberty, indeed she besought me, to write to our lord, the pope, certain resolutions, and she requested me to take an oath from my secretaries to keep silence.

Her discourses ranged from her first arrival in the kingdom till the present time. She affirmed, on her conscience, that from the 14th of November when she was first espoused to the late Prince Arthur, to the 2nd of April following, when he died, she did not sleep with him more than seven nights, and that she remained "intact as when she left the womb of her mother".

It does not seem likely that she will bend her resolve either one way or the other. (28 October 1528)

Campeggio to Sanga

In my most recent conversation with the lord cardinal he said and repeated many times in Latin: "Most reverend Lord, beware lest, in like manner as the greatest part of Germany has become estranged from the Apostolic See and from the Faith, it may be said that the same occasion is being given in England with the same result." Wolsey impresses upon me that if this divorce is not granted, the authority of the See Apostolic in this kingdom will be annihilated; and he certainly proves himself very zealous for its preservation, because all his grandeur is connected with it.

Thus I find myself in great straits, and with a heavy burden on my shoulders; nor do I see how judgement can be deferred even for a brief space. They will endure no procrastination, alleging that the affairs of the kingdom are at a standstill and dependent of the issue of this cause; and if it remains undetermined, it will give rise to infinite and imminent perils. (29 October 1528)

Henry VIII to Anne Boleyn

To inform you what joy it is to me to understand of your conformableness to reason, and of the suppressing of your inutile vain thoughts and fantasies with the bridle of reason, I ensure you all the good in this world could not counterpoise for my satisfaction the knowledge and certainty hereof. Wherefore, good sweetheart, continue in the same, not only in this but in all your doings hereafter; for thereby shall come, both to you and me, the greatest quietness that may be in this world. The cause why the bearer tarryeth so long is the business I have had to dress up for you, which I trust ere long to see you occupy, and then I trust to occupy yours, which shall be recompense enough to me for all my pains and labours. The unfeigned sickness of this well-willing legate doth somewhat retard his access to your presence; but I trust verily, when God shall send him health, he will with diligence recompense his delay, for I know well whereby he hath said it should be well known in this matter he is not Imperial. (31 October 1528)

JANUARY 1529 TO FEBRUARY 1529

Henry VIII and Wolsey were renowned and admired for their support of Christianity. The title Defender of the Faith was bestowed on Henry in 1521 by Pope Leo X for his defence of the Church against Lutheranism. He was a leader of the Church and his action to "dissolve" corrupt monasteries and redirect their excessive wealth for the purpose of building schools and more honest religious establishments was supported, particularly by the pope.

Queen Katherine had to call upon her nephew, Charles, to counter the formidable will of her husband and the vacillation of Pope Clement VII. Henry, however, now strengthens the group of

ambassadors he has sent to make sure this, or any future, pope acts
in his interest. Sir Francis Bryan was Anne Boleyn's cousin.

When a pope dies his successor is elected in secret concave by
the College of Cardinals.

Queen Katherine to Charles V

The king, having lately felt a scruple regarding the marriage between himself and her, has sought counsel of many
learned men, and finally has referred the matter to be
judged by the pope, who has given a commission to the
cardinal here, and another sent by his Holiness, for the purpose. Has exhibited to the king two copies, the one of a
bull, and the other of a brief, which were sent to her along
with the emperor's letters and signed by some of his secretaries. That of the bull agrees with the bull itself, which
is here; but, in the absence of the original brief, she is
informed by her counsel that the copy will not suffice to
be read before a judge. Begs him for the love of God to
help her to obtain justice. Is sure he would regret to see
her parted from her husband, and her child prejudiced. If
the brief were here, she could demand her rights by law.
Trusts the emperor, being so nearly related to her, will not
allow her to be dishonoured. Begs, therefore, that he will
send the original brief to the frontier of Bayonne, whence
the king will provide to have it conveyed safely through
France. The emperor may order a copy to be made according to law, by a judge ordinary or bishop, taking with him
a notary. Has given a procuration to the bearer, her chaplain, Thomas Abel, on this matter, and begs by all means to
have the original.

Begs his favour for Juan de Montoya, who goes to
conduct her chaplain through Spain, that he may go and
come freely. (Hampton Court, 9 January 1529)

Thomas Abel to Charles V

Is sent by the queen to desire of his majesty what may be most to her profit. She requests:

1   That his majesty in nowise give up the brief, notwithstanding that the queen's letter earnestly requests it, as she was compelled under oath to write in that manner.

2   That Charles should write to his ambassadors at Rome to use every effort to prevent the matter being examined anywhere but in Rome, for they have not yet begun to examine it in England; otherwise the queen's cause will be in great danger. If the pope reply that the queen herself has not asked it, the ambassador shall say that she neither says, nor writes, nor signs anything but what the king commands her; for to this she is compelled by a solemn oath.

3   The emperor's ambassadors should complain to the pope that he has given so many injunctions against the queen without having heard the parties, and should ask that he do not do so in future.

4   The emperor should send to England a good canonist as his ambassador, that he may, when needful, speak in the queen's business, as they cannot refuse to hear an ambassador, as they did those sent by Madame from Flanders, whom they ordered to return.

5   That Charles should order good canonists and legists to examine the matter, and write to the queen thereon something that she can make use of.

The divorce

Memorial of things to be said in answer to the emperor by the English ambassadors, if the matter of the king's marriage be touched upon and an appeal of the emperor be spoken of.

First, they must take care not to say anything about the case themselves; but if anything be said about it by the emperor or his councillors which calls for a reply either on the whole case or any part thereof, they are to adapt their answer thereto according to the following instructions:

1   If it be objected that the cause rests on no good foundation, but is instigated by some one in hatred to the emperor, after so many years, it will then be necessary to relate the origin and progress of the whole affair, how it came to light, how carefully it was examined at home and abroad, then referred to the pope, discussed at great length before him, and finally committed to be examined, viz., that whereas the king for some years past had noticed in reading the Bible the severe penalty inflicted by God on those who married the relicts of their brothers, he began to be troubled in his conscience, and to regard the sudden deaths of his male children as a divine judgement. The more he studied the matter, the more clearly it appeared to him that he had broken a divine law. He then called to counsel men learned in pontifical law, to ascertain their opinion of the dispensation. Several pronounced it invalid. So far he had proceeded as secretly as possible, that he might do nothing rashly. He then assembled the bishops of England, and the most learned men both in divine and human law, by whom with mature deliberation all that could be said both for and against the marriage was epitomised in one volume. By common consent the cause was declared one for the pope's judgement, and the king accordingly sent ambassadors to the pope with the book containing the merits of the case. The matter was discussed before the pope by Simonetta, dean of the rota, Cardinals Monte and SS Quatuor and Dr Capasuk,

auditor of the rota, and afterwards by Vincent de Perusio. On being pressed to declare their opinions, the pope asked the ambassadors instead if they would undertake a general commission to be executed in England, and he would confirm the sentence. After long intercession, the ambassadors, finding there was no hope of getting the pope to pronounce an opinion, addressed his Holiness, telling him that it was apparent he either would not or could not pronounce an opinion; that if he could not, people would think God had taken from him the key of knowledge, and that pontifical laws which were not clear to the pope himself deserved to be committed to the flames, as they had been elsewhere; but that if he could and would not do what he ought to do willingly, viz., show an erring man the way, it was gross dereliction of his functions. And they urged the pope not to be wanting to a prince to whom he confessed himself under such obligations. To this his Holiness replied only by asking them to be content with a general commission, and not insist upon a direct sentence. The ambassadors then told the pope that he did in fact the very thing he would not in words; for what was granting a commission but an acknowledgement, in part, of the goodness of the cause? At last the ambassadors had to accept a commission to Cardinals Wolsey and Campeggio, and returned. Thus it is evident every step has been taken which behoved for the proper cognisance of the cause before the pope himself; nor would the king have been at so much trouble and expense if he had only cared to indulge his own desires.

2   If only parts of the case be touched upon, as whether such marriages are prohibited by divine law, a little book has been drawn up, the arguments of which might be briefly referred to. Reasons adduced to show

that the prohibition in Leviticus XVIII applies to the wife of a deceased as well as of a living brother.

3   If the papal dispensation be alleged, it may be replied that many learned men doubt the power of the pope to dispense, and all agree that he cannot do so except for the most urgent causes, which are not found in the bull of Julius.

4   If mention be made of the brief which is with the emperor: there are grave suspicions about this brief, which, even if taken separately they be insufficient; collectively they are of great force. First, there is no entry of it in the registers at Rome. Second, it is not in England, where it ought to be. Third, it appears to have the same date as the bull, and it is extremely unlikely that a bull and brief should both be issued the same day about the same cause, or that a dispensation under wax should be more efficacious than one under lead. Fourth, it corrects the errors in the bull which have lately been brought to light, and that to a quite unnecessary extent, as in omitting the word *forsan* lest it should suggest a doubt. Fifth, it is not dated according to the computation used in papal briefs, by which the year begins at Christmas; for, according to that computation, the date is before Julius became pope.

5   If it be said these arguments reflect dishonour on the emperor, as he who uses a forged document is no less guilty than a forger, it may be replied that the king quite acquits the emperor of all intentional error in the matter, as he might easily have been imposed upon.

6   If anything be said of sending the brief to England: there are many reasons why it should be sent. First, it properly belongs to the king and queen, to whom it is addressed, not to the emperor. Second, it concerns them to have true and valid dispensations. Third, when

the cause was heard in England, messengers from the queen were sent to Spain to procure the original and not a transcript, that in such an important case the judges might decide with their own eyes; and though the emperor might allege that it was in danger of being lost by the way, the loss would not concern him, but the king and queen. The emperor, no doubt, had good reason for sending only a copy when peace was not firmly established, but the king has no doubt he will send the original now in proof of his friendship to the king.

7   If the emperor say the king's cause ought not to be judged in his own kingdom, it is to be answered, first, that the pope has judged otherwise, as the emperor's ambassador related the whole affair from the beginning. Second, what place could be more convenient for an examination of noblemen and other witnesses, and for an exhibition of documents which it would not be right to take out of the kingdom? The only real objection to such a course, viz., the power of a prince in his own kingdom, ceases in this case, as the king has always submitted himself freely to judgement, and allowed the queen both foreign and English counsel. Third, if England be an unsuitable place, how much less suitable is Rome, which was in the power of the emperor, and is not even yet free.

Wm Goldwin, master of the school at Ipswich, to Wolsey
Expresses his gratitude and that of the people of Ipswich. Sends specimens of the handwriting of some of the boys, who, he hopes, will soon be able to speak Italian. The number is increasing, so that the schoolhouse is becoming too small. (4 January 1529)

Sir Gregory Casale to —

On the 8th I wrote to you that the pope was unwell. Since then his illness has increased so greatly that fears arose of his death; which God forbid in these turbulent times. Last night he took some medicine, which has produced little effect. This evening we have received some hope of his recovery, as the fever has not returned at its usual term; but he is not yet out of danger. Yester even the pope held a consistory, and created the magnifico Hippolito a cardinal. (Rome, 11 January 1529)

Sir Gregory Casale to —

Last night the pope had a return of the fever. Cause the mandate or proxy to be sent with all the clauses, especially that for extinguishing and compounding the pension. (Rome, 12 January 1529)

Paul Casale to —

Hears that the pope has been ill of a fever. Towards evening he was slightly relieved and took supper, which he could not retain on his stomach. This, however, augurs well for his recovery; but some regard it as a bad sign. (Rome, 12 January 1529)

Lee to Wolsey

I beg you will remember your words when I took my leave of you at Hampton Court, and that the things now committed to our charge may be concluded one way or other. As the voice runs that the emperor will go into Italy, I beg I may not have to follow him. (Valladolid, 15 January 1529)

Inigo di Mendoza to Charles V

The king and his council attach so much importance to the brief that the emperor has, that they are trying by every means to get it into their hands. The king has made the queen swear that she will do all she can to procure it, for which purpose she has been made to write a letter and protestation addressed to the emperor, quite against her own will. However, she has sent a messenger named Montoya, instructed by word of mouth, to inform his majesty of the whole affair. It was dangerous to give him a cipher, lest it should awake suspicion in France. Suggests that a copy of the brief be made in the presence of the English ambassadors and some bishops, for the confusion of those who take Henry's part. Hears from Rome of the supplication and protestation made by the ambassador to the pope about this matter.

Three days ago there arrived a messenger from the pope, and another from the king of England's ambassador there, and, so far as I can understand, the pope does not mean to give a mandate for settling the cause here.

The king has told me that he has begun to lay the blame upon his cardinal, who, he says, has not fulfilled his promises in the matter. All that he has done about it hitherto has been to desire the pope and the king to frighten the queen, so that she should of her own accord enter religion; nevertheless, he has secretly intimated to this legate (Campeggio) that if she refuse, no further use shall be made of the commission which he publicly bears without a new mandate. The ambassador, moreover, writes from Rome that if the queen had sent power to make the same demand on her own account that he has done on behalf of the emperor, the cause would already have been revoked to Rome.

Has done his best to solicit the queen to this effect. But she neither can nor dare do it. Nevertheless, I think she will write in her own hand to the pope, by which her wish may appear.

Wolsey is very ill pleased that the English ambassadors are away from the court, but the less he likes it the more reason there is for keeping them at a distance. Perhaps it would even be better if they were out of the kingdom.

The collector who came from Spain has reported that he had been told by persons of authority that, if this war goes on, your majesty might make a new king of England; and such was the fear they showed that the cardinal told them in public that, in order to irritate the English against the emperor, he had conceded to them one thing that they had long asked for—that foreigners should not be allowed to keep any household except with English workmen—and that a number of Flemings had already been compelled to depart.

Nothing is more necessary than that the queen should get the cause revoked to Rome, as neither she nor the judges are free.

Wolsey to a cardinal at Rome

They are making great efforts to have a sight of the original brief in order to pronounce some decision upon it. For that purpose the queen has been induced to send to the emperor to ask for it in her own name. He is to entreat the pope to write to the emperor, and demand the production of the original within a given time, as delays are prejudicial and great suspicions exist. They are anxious to have their own opinion of the matter justified, and if your lordship can do anything towards augmenting those suspicions, and make the truth appear, the king will be most grateful to you. You may be supplied with any sum of money necessary for prosecuting the inquiry and discovering how this brief was procured. To delay sentence on a vain and suspicious brief is unjust and perilous to this kingdom.

Clement VII to Campeggio

Whereas it has come to the pope's knowledge that the whole controversy of the divorce has turned upon the insufficiency of the dispensation found in the English state paper office, and that the queen has exhibited the copy of a brief, of which the original is in Spain, but not found in England, respecting the genuineness of which great doubts are entertained; we authorise you to reject whatever evidence is tendered in behalf of this brief as an evident forgery, and to proceed according to the tenor of our previous letters.

Stephen Gardiner to Thomas Arundel

Gentle Master Arundel, by these letters I shall take you by the hand, and bid you most heartily farewell, supplying that which I could not yesterday do, as well for that ye waiting upon my lord's grace, and I hasted to repair hither, were suddenly sundered, as also that in very deed my stomach would not suffer me so to do; but though I depart from you in body, I depart not in mind and soul, which, considering it may be where I list, ye may be well assured it shall be ever where you be during my life, wheresoever this body shall fortune to wander. As knoweth God, who send you most heartily well to fare. At Westminster, this morning. Entirely your own, Stephen Gardiner.

Paul Casale to his brother the prothonotary

After you left we were all thrown into confusion, from fright of the death of the pope. His Holiness was in such extremity that one night, about 8, the physicians, finding no pulse, gave him over for dead. Next morning he recovered. The disease is so diminished that the fever has now left him, and tonight his physicians will give him a purge. In the tumult Hippolito de Medici was created cardinal, much against the wish of the pope, and has the archbishopric of Avignon. Doria was created cardinal by some intrigue. Bryan and Vannes, the English ambassadors, have arrived. Two others are expected. The famine is bad here. (Rome, 19 January 1529)

Henry VIII to Jacobo Salviati

Has heard from his ambassadors and others of Salviati's zeal for his service. Means to write to him frequently. Is sending Stephen Gardiner, LL.D., to the pope, and has commissioned him to confer with Salviati on matters which concern the king's health of soul and body, the security of his kingdom and the honour of the papal See. (Hamptoncorte, 20 January 1529)

John Casale to Wolsey

The pope is dead. He was in good health when Casale left Rome. He was taken ill at mass on the Epiphany, as Wolsey will see by the enclosed letters. Received today letters from the duke of Urbino from Pesaro, saying that he was dead. Will write more fully by the next courier. Is sorry he left the city, for he might have done something to prevent the election of an Imperialist.

However, his two brothers will do their best, and also Peter Vannes and his companion, whom he supposes to be at Rome, as they left Bologna on the 7th. Italian affairs are in the same state as at the departure of his cousin Vincent, except what has happened at Aquila, of which he encloses an account. (Venice, 21 January 1529)

Gardiner to Wolsey

This Friday morning, wind and tide being favourable, I embarked for Calais, intending to go on with all diligence to Paris and there await my letters. (Dover, Friday, 22 January 1529)

Du Bellay to Montmorency

While waiting to close his packet at the departure of the tide (*au partment de la marée*), learned from a good authority that the charge of Dr Stephen is, among other things, to tell the pope that if he do not make Campeggio proceed with this divorce and despatch the matter, the king of England will throw off his allegiance. This, I am told, is quite certain, and it agrees with what I wrote to you. Campeggio came upon me today by surprise at my lodging, where, having leisure to speak to him apart, I tried to probe him on this matter, but I see he dare not speak, so I suspect that Dr Stephen will not have told you everything either; but, at all events, I thought it right to tell you all I have been able to make out. Wolsey is in great difficulty, for the affair has gone so far that if it do not take effect, the king will fall out with him, and if he do, he will have to carry it with a strong hand. Chayney had offended Wolsey some days ago and had been put out of the court. The young lady has put him in again, and used very rude words of Wolsey. Think what may be the effect of this. The duke of Norfolk and his party already begin to talk big, but certainly they have to do with one more subtle than themselves.

Katherine of Aragon to Muscetula

Has received his letter with the other writings. Thanks him for his diligence in her service, and begs him to continue. Wishes to know what answer the pope made to his petitions. Will commend his services to the emperor. Desires credence for Inigo di Mendoza. (Hampton Court, 25 January 1529)

Inigo di Mendoza to Muscetula

Has received three letters from him, the last dated on the 13th ult. and also the protestation and supplication made in the queen's matter. Muscetula could not have done better. His advice that the queen should apply to get the cause revoked to Rome would have been taken long ago if it had been possible; but she can do nothing but what her husband desires. His Holiness, however, should see that in this kingdom she cannot defend herself, and for the honour of the Church the case should not be allowed to be decided out of Rome. The pope has always written to his legate, as you have informed us, that, not being able to draw the queen into religion, the case should be suspended until he receive a new mandate from his Holiness.

A draft letter has been prepared with much trouble and difficulty, which the queen may write with her own hand to the pope, expressing her free will, on which I hope the cause will be removed to Rome.

Arrangements for communicating through Cardinal Sanctae Crucis.

The queen had two dispensations from Pope Julius. Of the first and principal, the king has here an authentic copy, as the emperor also has in Spain, but of the second they have none in England, and they will use every effort to get it from the emperor; but his majesty will, of course, take great care not to give it up, as in it consists the whole of the queen's right. If the original or the register can be discovered at Rome, it would be well to get an authentic extract, or at least get it examined.

The queen was compelled some days past to swear solemnly that she would use every effort to get the brief which the emperor has, and they have made her write to the emperor for it as urgently as if her life depended on it; but his majesty must be informed that this was done entirely under compulsion.

Bids him inform the Cardinal Sanctae Crucis that he has intelligence that the kings of France and England and the cardinal make great suit to the pope that he should go to Avignon, where they offer to go themselves, so as to arrange matters that the emperor's journey into Italy may be prevented. (London, 25 January 1529)

Cardinal Wolsey to the earl of Beaumont (Montmorency)

Having begun to build two colleges—one at Ipswich, which is the place of my birth, and the other in the university of Oxford, where scholars shall be brought up in virtue, and qualified for the sacerdotal dignity—which edifices cannot be properly completed because we have not here in abundance the stone which you have there; for this reason I pray you very earnestly to be a means with the king your master that he will do me the honour to assign to me a quarry at Caen, in Lower Normandy, and that leave may be given to my people there to take and carry away all such stone as shall be necessary for the perfection of the said edifices, without paying any duty thereupon. (Richmond, 26 January 1529)

Bryan to Henry VIII

Since my last from Florence of the 9th, I have heard that the pope was very sick. Remembering your letters and the money, I determined to leave them with Vannes at Orvieto and go with Penyson to Rome. When we came to Orvieto, heard the pope was not dead; so we rode to Viterbo, till we came to Ronsylyon, where I delivered to Cardinal Farnese your letter. We dined with him, and think he is your friend. He offered us horses to Tome, and on the way we were met by certain horsemen sent by Master Gregory Casale. He is a marvellous good servant to your grace. If you would reward his brother, who is your ambassador at Venice, with some abbey, it would redound to your honour. We have been here 12 days, and cannot speak with the pope. If he had died there would have been a mischievous business. If he die, Master Gregory has made incredible efforts for us to have a pope in our favour.

We have searched all the registers and can find no brief. We have written to the Wolsey about it. Before we speak with the pope, which will not be before 12 days, we shall do the best we can in your cause, both for the charge we brought with us, and what Thaddeus brought since. There has been a great to-do about making cardinals.

Gives an account of the dispute about the making of Cardinal Doria. Speaks highly of the Cardinal of Mantua (Gonzaga), who is very fond of hunting. Report of the death of Andrea Doria.

This is the third letter I have sent. It is reported here that Campeggio is thoroughly Imperial, and for your matter there could not have been a worse one sent. Vannes is very diligent. (Rome, 26 January 1529)

John Casale to Wolsey

Although I wrote that the duke of Urbino had notified the pope's death, the pope was still alive, although given over for dead.

Excuses himself for giving false intelligence. (Venice, 26 January 1529)

Count De Carpi to Mgr —

Yesterday, the treasurer, Grollier, spoke to me from you of the present occurrences, desiring me to give my opinion to Francis and you, what should be done in case of the pope's death. I gave him my opinion by word of mouth, but I think it right to draw up this little memorandum also, as my illness will not permit me to go to the king and you myself. The treasurer also assured me on your part that you would take good order about my private business, though you had not been able to see to it yet. Thanks him for this intimation. (Paris, 2 February 1529)

1   Roll of the cardinals who will be of the opposite party.
2   Cardinals who may be gained by one or other party.
3   Absent cardinals.

4 Opinion above referred to: Thinks Francis should write to the Sacred College, offering all his forces for the protection of the church, and to secure the freedom of the election. The French ambassadors also should be instructed to hold like language, and, if they find the Imperialists inclined to use force, protest to the college that they should refuse to enter the conclave, or come out after they have entered, and retire to some place where they can conduct the election in surety.

Gregory Casale and Peter Vannes to Wolsey

Write in great haste by a person who is going to the count of St Pôl. Hear from a sure and secret quarter that the pope's disease has increased to delirium and vomiting, and his life is despaired of.

Does all that the king and Wolsey could expect from any one. Have written to St Pôl to ask the French king to send the French cardinals to the frontiers, for unless the new pope is created by our faction the French will be able to do nothing. Cardinals Triulzi and Pisano, who have been lately released, are coming hither. (Rome, 3 February 1529)

Inigo di Mendoza to Charles V

Wrote in his last how the queen had been compelled to send a messenger with a letter under her hand for the brief which is in the emperor's possession. The messenger whom she first sent, by name Françoise Philippe, was obliged to return, and the queen sent two others, one of whom she did not trust, and accordingly she sent with him a Spaniard, named Montoya, by sea.

They attach much more importance here to the brief which the emperor has than to the dispensation, and do all they can to get hold of it. I believe they have word from

Rome that it is not found in the register, so it must be kept all the more securely, and care must be taken, even in giving a copy, that there be no mistake about it. It would be very desirable that it should be seen by the English ambassadors before it is used.

Has received from the ambassador at Rome the protestation made upon this subject. Thinks he has used every effort to get the cause revoked to Rome. For this it is expedient that the queen should send a power to decline this tribunal, or at least a letter under her hand, by which her will might be apparent. The power cannot be sent, because the queen is surrounded by spies in her own chamber. The letter she may find a place to write, although with great difficulty, by which the pope will see alike the little liberty she is allowed, and that she approves of the requests made on her behalf by the emperor's ambassador.

Thinks this will be sufficient to silence these judges and get the cause removed into the consistory. Campeggio has always written hitherto, notwithstanding his commission, that proceedings shall in no wise commence here until he receives a new mandate; and the king, knowing this, has sent a gentleman of his chamber, and a learned man, to the pope to press the matter. Believes the emperor's just favour will weigh more than their unjust demands.

This lady, who is the cause of all the disorder, finding her marriage delayed, that she thought herself so sure of, entertains great suspicion that this cardinal of England puts impediments in her way, from a belief that if she were queen his power would decline. In this suspicion she is joined by her father, and the two dukes of Suffolk and Norfolk, who have combined to overthrow the cardinal; but as yet they have made no impression on the king, except that he shows him in court not quite so good countenance as he did, and that he has said some disagreeable words to him.

Is informed that the French king with this king and the cardinal have urged the pope to go to Avignon, where they will all meet and arrange to stop the emperor's going to Italy. Has not been able to learn the pope's answer. Has given notice to the emperor's ambassador in Rome by cipher.

Every day matters turn up about the queen, for which it is needful to dispatch couriers to Rome, but she has so little liberty that she is unable to find a messenger, and refers everything to me; nor can I myself do anything but send the despatches to M Hochstrat, to whom I request you will write to use all diligence in sending couriers.

Has just heard that the king has pressed the legates so urgently to have the cause decided here that they have sent two secretaries to the pope, and have given the king great hope of a favourable answer. The king is so hot upon it that there is nothing he does not promise to gain his end; and if the cause be tried here it may be considered as lost, for I have as little trust in the new legate as in the old one. Campeggio has done nothing for the queen as yet, except to press her to enter religion.

The emperor has done well to keep the ambassadors at a distance from the court, notwithstanding Wolsey's complaints of it, as their only occupation is to write what passes.

This letter has been written seven days, the ship having been detained longer than he expected.

News has come through France that the pope is dead. Does not know if it is true, but has no doubt it has disconcerted them here, as they expected the pope would be forced to comply with their wishes. It was told him by the queen; and if it is not true, it is the fault of the French. (London, 4 February 1529)

Paul Casale to Vincent Casale

The pope has pretty well recovered. As he could not take the purge nor retain any medicine, his physicians gave him four or five pills, which produced great evacuation; but on the day when he was thought to be better, he was again attacked by the fever, worse than usual, and was in great pain all night, with frequent vomiting and paroxysms in the head. His fever is very bad again today. They have great apprehensions about him. The Imperial ambassador has offered the citadel of Ostia etc. to the college of cardinals, on payment of 6,000 Spanish crowns. (Rome, 4 February 1529)

Abstinence of war

Notification by the emperor to the council of Flanders that the abstinence of war between himself and the kings of France and England, concluded for eight months from the 15th of last June, will endure until one of the contracting parties proclaims his intention to keep it no longer, giving two months' notice for the safety of merchants. (Malines, 4 February 1529)

Charles V to the bishop of Burgos

Hears by various ways of the urgent efforts made by the king of England to obtain a divorce from his queen, the emperor's aunt; a thing which grieves him deeply, especially in the present scandalous state of the Christian commonwealth. Believes it must arise from the sinister persuasions of some who are about him. Has no doubts it will grieve all good subjects to the kingdom who know that this marriage was made by express permission of the Holy See and has remained unquestioned so many years. The emperor is compelled for his part to support his aunt, and has given charge to his ambassadors accordingly. He has also prayed the pope that the cause may be determined in consistory, and not in England. Desires the bishop to labour in this behalf in the queen's name at Rome. (Toledo, 6 February 1529)

Instructions to Gardiner, Bryan, Gregory Casale and Vannes at Rome

Since the departure of Gardiner the king has by sundry ways been advertised of the pope's death, so that the charge committed to them cannot be executed. Considering the dissensions among Christian princes, and the prospect of the ruin of the See Apostolic unless the ambition of those who wish to exterminate it is repressed by the help of good and virtuous princes, it is necessary that such a head and common father should be chosen as can and will provide for the restoration of the Holy See, will have the assistance of virtuous princes and can resist the inordinate ambition of the emperor, who studies for his own exaltation to suppress the Church. The king's matrimonial cause, which has been committed to them, delay in which would bring manifold dangers, can only be settled by the special favour of the head of the Church; and he is loth to recur to any remedy except the authority of the See Apostolic, if he can find there favour answering to his merits, of which favour he would be clearly deprived if the future pope were a person of whom he was not perfectly assured. The French king is thoroughly united to him. When all the cardinals are considered, none can be found furnished with the requisites before named except Wolsey, who is well known to have as fervent zeal as any person for the tranquillity of Christendom, the restoration of the authority and rights of the Church and the See Apostolic, the weal and exaltation of the kings of England and France and their allies, and also for the perfection of the king's cause.

The French king has spontaneously offered to use his influence on his behalf. He is the only person who can cope with the inordinate ambition of the emperor, establish tranquillity in Christendom and prevent the injury which will ensue to the Church from the passage of the emperor to Rome next January. The king expects that the emperor will endeavour to obtain the election of a pope who is devoted to him, and take from him all the rights and patrimony of the Church, using him as his vassal and chaplain, or else by little and little "extinct" him and his authority. The king desires them, therefore, to use every means to advance Wolsey's election, as that on which depends the making or marring of the king's cause.

If the future pope were an enemy to the king, it would be impossible to obtain the king's desire. If he were indifferent, he would get nothing but fair words and delay, as has already been seen in one who had more cause to adhere to the king than to be indifferent. A list is enclosed of the cardinals likely to be absent and present at the election. The names of those favourable to the kings of England and France are marked with "a", the Imperialists "e" and the neutrals "n". Thirty-nine cardinals are expected to be present, and it will be sufficient to gain 26. Twenty are thought to be friendly, so that six only need be gained. If the cardinals present, having God and the Holy Ghost before them, consider what is best for the Church, they cannot fail to agree upon Wolsey; but as human fragility suffers not all things to be weighed in just balances, the ambassadors are to make promises of spiritual promotions, offices, dignities, rewards of money and other things, to show them what Wolsey will give up if he enters into this dangerous storm and troublous tempest for the relief of the Church; all of which benefices shall be given to the king's friends, besides other large rewards. The ambassadors are furnished with a commission for this purpose, and letters to the college of cardinals, and particular cardinals, which they are to deliver. By promises and arguments they must firmly unite a band of 20, 18 or at least 16 cardinals, who will prevent any adverse party from gaining the election, and make the residue more ready to come over to their side. But if any for private ambition persist in contending for themselves, it is evident that they are seeking the ruin of the See Apostolic, and the ambassadors must find means to have some sure persons in the conclave to practise what is necessary, and to send information to them so that they may know how to act. Suggests that De Vaulx should be one to enter the conclave; that Gregory Casale should do the like. As this election by one way or other suffereth no negative, if for lack of grace or entendement there should be any despair thereof, the ambassadors are to publish a protestation passed by the cardinals in England and France, of which a copy is enclosed. This may beforehand be couched and devised by Gardiner, and set forth by the policy of De Vaulx and Casale. The cardinals on the English and French side will then leave the conclave, repair to some sure place and proceed with the election, notwithstanding any election that may ensue at Rome.

The ambassadors may offer the cardinals a guard of 2,000 or 3,000 men, to be in Rome during the election; and if the offer is accepted, they must take money by exchange and provide the men. The French king has ordered Renzio to lie between the army of Naples and Rome, and the viscount of Turenne and the Venetians will lie on the other side, so that they will be free from fear of the Imperialists.

The cardinals need not fear that Wolsey would reside at Avignon or other place away from Rome. For, first, he would resign all his dignities, and have no convenient habitation except Rome; and, second, the reason of his desiring the papacy is his zeal for the Church, and he would therefore proceed directly to his See. The ambassadors are to use all means to gain the Venetians, the Florentines, the duke of Ferrara and others. They must assure the adherents of the Medici of Wolsey's favour; the Florentines, of their freedom; the cardinals, of the recovery of the patrimonies of the Church; and the Venetians, of a reasonable settlement concerning Cervia and Ravenna. They must show the duke of Ferrara that Wolsey was the means of his alliance with the French king, and promise the continuance of his favour.

Bids them have regard to the conduct of the French ambassadors, lest, despairing of the advancement of Wolsey, they incline to some other cardinal and refuse to make the protestation. Desires them to assure the cardinals that, if the Imperialists proceed to an election without the consent of the residue, no prince will favour them except the emperor and his brother. The king would consent to the election of the Cardinal Campeggio if the election of Wolsey were impossible. (Signed by the king at the beginning and the end. In the hand of Vannes.)

Wolsey to Sir Gregory Casale and Peter Vannes

Laments the death of the pope. It is of the utmost importance that they see no one elected who is hostile to the king of England. Leaves to their dexterity and fidelity what they are to do for the promotion of himself. They will gather this from his letters. (London, 6 February 1529)

Wolsey to Gardiner

Although they are sufficiently informed, by the instructions given to Mgr Vincent, of the king's and his intention concerning his advancement to the papacy, writes these few words to him as the person whom he most trusts, and by whom this matter will be most set forth. Doubts not that he considers the state of the Church and all Christendom, and also of this realm, which would be utterly undone if the king's secret matter were settled in any other way than by the authority of the Church. It is therefore expedient to have such a person for pope and common father to all princes as will apply a remedy; and although Wolsey considers himself unsuitable on account of his old age, yet, when all the cardinals are considered, there will be found none who can and will set a remedy in the aforesaid things, except himself. If it were not for the restoration of the Church and the See Apostolic to their former dignity, and for the sake of obtaining peace amongst Christian princes and relieving England from its present calamities, would never accept the papacy; but, in accordance with the necessity of the time and the will of these two kings, will do all he can to attain this dignity. Wishes him therefore to use all his power, and spare no expense, promises or labour to bring this to pass, and to act according as he sees how persons are inclined. He and his colleagues have most ample power. Leaves everything to his skill and faithfulness. (Westminster, 7 February 1529)

Lee to Henry VIII

On the same subject as the preceding: Some think the delay of the emperor's journey is in consequence of his doubt of the king; and some think for the loyalty of this country, if he left it. Another cause suggested is lack of money.

There is much clamour for wages, which are in arrears for two or three years. Some of the Burgonion guard have gone home. (Valladolid, 9 February 1529)

Charles V to the council and nobles of Guipuscoa

Declares his desire for peace, and the danger in which Naples is of being overrun by the Turks. Is going to Barcelona and leaves his empress and Philip and Mary, his children, to govern these kingdoms. Intends to offer the

French king new terms which he cannot honourably refuse, and will stay at Barcelona until he has fresh news, when he will go to Italy, if necessary. Desires them to maintain order during his absence. (Toledo, 20 February 1529)

Henry VIII to Clement VII

Is gratified at finding how much his efforts in behalf of the knights of St John have been set forth in the pope's breve. Has resolved to give the Order 20,000 crowns. (Greenwich, 25 February 1529)

MARCH 1529

Henry took elaborate steps to ensure that the pope took the course of action he desired. He applied constant pressure through his ambassadors in Rome. He pursued the legal invalidity of documents in Spain, endeavoured to make sure that Charles did not go to the pope and made sure that no assistance could get to the queen. In all these precautions he was assisted by Anne Boleyn, to whom he had clearly promised that there would be a divorce.

Charles V to Mai

The king of England has sent hither to obtain from him the dispensation granted for his marriage with the queen.

The queen also, at his desire, has written and sent him a chaplain of hers. Is assured that she has done this under constraint, and that she writes at the king's dictation, both to this court and to other parts. They have also made her swear that she will not write anything in this matter without the king's knowledge. Two lawyers sent into England by Madame Margaret to defend the queen's cause have been ordered out of the kingdom, so that she is not at liberty to do anything in her own cause. It is therefore right that his Holiness should revoke Campeggio's commission at the emperor's request, as a person related to her, and recall the cause to Rome. Mai had better consult the Cardinal Sanctae Crucis about it. (Toledo, 3 March 1529)

Cloth of gold for the wardrobe

Bond given by John Francis Reiner de Bardi and his partners Francis de Bardi, John de Bardi, John Baptist de Caponis and Jacobus de Caponis, merchants of Florence, to Wolsey and Brian Tuke, in 10,294*l*. 0*s*. 14*d*., for the delivery into the king's great wardrobe, beside the Blackfriars, London, during 26 years coming, in payment of 10,294*l*. 0*s*. 14*d*. according to 26 several obligations, of cloths of gold, velvets, satins, and other silks, according to an indenture of 3rd September. (20 Henry VIII. 3 March 1529)

Mai to Charles V

This day, the 6th March, I received an enclosure from the ambassador in England, dated the 25th ult., who writes in reply to a letter of mine, declaring how tenderly your majesty had desired me to look after the affairs of the queen. I also received a letter from her highness on the same subject. As we had written to her that it was needful the queen or someone in her name should make an appeal that the cause should be removed to Rome, and as they write that the queen is not in such liberty as it would be needful, they have arranged here with great difficulty that the queen should write to the pope in her own hand declaring her wish; and she writes to me to give the letter to the pope very secretly, for it must on no account be known. The pope is not yet well enough to transact business, but when he is I will give him the letter. (Rome, 16 March 1529)

Gardiner, Bryan and Vannes to Wolsey

The French kindly wrote a letter of credence to Bryan, which was delivered to him by the French ambassador, who told him that the French king thanked him for the good account he had given of him to the allies, and for what he had said of the indissoluble friendship between him and Henry. He then said, as of himself, that he thought it his duty to tell Bryan that he had heard that he and his colleagues had offered in the king's name a great sum of money to the emperor for his consent in the king's cause, and that the Imperialists boasted that they would obtain money on this pretext, and that the king would in the end be deluded by the pope. Said that this was an idle story, and that the king, trusting in the justice of his cause, had forbidden them to make any offers to anyone; and asked him to refer to his colleagues, which at length he did.

Believes that some one has written thus to Francis to make him suspect that the king wishes to come to an agreement with the emperor. Tells this to Wolsey that he may clear the king from the suspicion if he think it necessary. The pope gave a hint to this effect to Gardiner and Vannes, and said that he was surprised that the emperor had not offered peace to the king if the queen could be persuaded to enter religion. Said that the friendship between the kings of England and France was indissoluble. His Holiness replied that it was not expedient that this friendship should be dissolved while the emperor was so powerful. Said that the friendship was perpetual, and that they could not talk of this. Do not know whether the emperor or the pope have commenced such practices, or whether anyone else has written about it to the French king. Send the credential letters of the French king.

Wolsey to Gardiner, Bryan, Gregory Casale and Vannes
Yesterday, while he was with the king, their letters of the 3rd and 21st arrived. Has not received their letters of the 14th with the bulls for Winchester. Desires them to find out what has become of them. Has made a fresh arrangement with Vivalde for the money. The king received yesterday letters from the bishop of Worcester and Mr Almoner, dated the 12th ult., stating that the nuncio who was resident in Spain is dead. Encloses a copy of the letter. The pope's rescripts to the emperor for exhibition of the original brief here or at Rome must therefore be sent to some other person favourable to the king's cause. Desired Gardiner to write to the bishop and Almoner that they may make the certificates accordingly, and also to endeavour to procure the appointment of a nuncio of another sort than the late one, whose death they think will be no "demore" to the king's cause. The king and he are glad to hear of the pope's recovery, and hope they have already been with him.

The letters sent by Casale and Hercules (Missolus) will tell them what to do if the pope dies. Doubts the truth of their reports about the strength of the Imperialists. The friendly cardinals must be the more solicited to look unto themselves, lest they fall into the power of the Imperialists.

The emperor's ambassador has just brought to the queen a transumpt of the brief alleged to be in the emperor's hands, passed by the archbishop of Toledo and the late nuncio. Encloses a copy. The king summoned his council to decide upon the efficacy of the transumpt, and divers notable defaults have been found in it, which give more suspicion than ever. Sends a book giving the particulars of these faults. The pope or any other person will easily see that all is craft, colour and falsity, and that by making the transumpt before it is required, and in an insufficient manner, they intend to prevent their being called upon to show the original. All this they are to show to the pope. As they have gone about to supply the defaults of the bull by a brief alleged to be in their hands, they in manner confess the bull to be of no effect. Their recurring to the allegation of a thing forged, feigned and untrue, is a proof that the whole matter of matrimony is void and of none effect. The pope, therefore, while God gives him time, should put an end to this just cause, lest, wilfully, suffering a thing of such high importance to be unreformed, to the doing whereof Almighty God worketh so openly, he should incur God's displeasure. They must remind him of the danger to his soul if he die without reforming it. Charges them to see the matter speedily and effectually executed.

The errors in the brief in writing the king's name, his father's, the queen's and Prince Arthur's make the king and all other wise men here think it is forged; for no person can think that such errors could pass the secretaries or the chancery, especially as Sigismunde was a man of such experience, and no such errors are found in his writings. It is thought that the pope can make no reasonable difficulty in the matter.

Fears that the letters with the bulls of Winchester have miscarried, and desires them to send duplicates.

The king hears from his ambassadors in Spain that the emperor's voyage into Italy is laid asleep for this year, and that the biscuit and other victuals provided for the voyage are put to sale. Wishes them to inform the pope thereof.

The French king is making fresh preparations to invade Spain, and has gone towards Blois. He intends to reinforce his armies in Naples and Milan, that the pope may the less regard the emperor's power, and have the better commodity to bring about a peace at the convention. (Hampton Court, 14 March 1529)

The divorce

Julius was created pope November 1 and crowned 26 November 1503. In the date of the brief the year is computed from Christmas, which is an error. The brief should have contained the clause *non obstantibus constitutionibus et ordinationibus apostolicis*, especially as there is a constitution of a general council against such a dispensation. The brief could, however, be sustained without this clause. A king is styled "dilecto filio in Christo, Henrico, etc." a king's son or other prince "dilecto filio Henrico". There is no absolution from censures, which is commonly placed in apostolic letters, though sometimes omitted in briefs. The clause is omitted, *proviso quod tu, filia, propter hoc rapta non fueris*, which is commonly inserted in letters apostolic, though sometimes omitted in briefs.

If the queen intends to make use of the dispensation granted to her by brief by Julius II, the original must be produced, that its genuineness may be investigated:

1   It must be examined in the sunlight to see if there are any erasures.
2   Whether anything has been obliterated and rewritten.
3   Whether paper has been gummed over an erasure.
4   Whether letters and words are more distinct in one place than in another, or there is any blemish in the paper.
5   The seal of the fisherman must be compared with other seals of Pope Julius.

6 Whether the whole brief is written in the same hand, and whether the last line is complete.

7 Whether the secretary's signature is in the usual place.

8 Whether the paper is old, and whether the brief is according to the style of the court of Rome.

9 Whether there is any false Latinity or other discrepancy.

10 Compare the style and the letters.

11 Search for a copy in the register.

12 Ask the advice of advocates learned in the style of the court.

13 Advise the pope to use his authority to discover the truth.

To ascertain whether there is any error in the date of the brief, it must be considered whether in briefs the year is computed from Christmas. If so, there is a manifest error, for the date is 26 December 1503, in the name of Pope Julius, who was not created pope until 1 November 1503, 10 months later. It is of no avail to say that the year has been computed in the brief from the incarnation, for that is contrary to the style of the court of Rome, and is a manifest error, which gives treat suspicion of forgery. Even if this error were not sufficient alone to cause a suspicion of forgery, it assuredly is so when joined with the other errors in the brief.

As a bull is of more power than a brief, and not much more expensive, it is unlikely that for a matter of such importance a brief should have been obtained, and it is much more probable that it has been lately concocted to exclude the only exception in the bull.

The divorce

Summary of the reasons which should persuade the pope to pronounce sentence for the king in the matter of the divorce.

The marriage is contrary to divine and human law. If the papal dispensation is put forward as an argument, it may be answered that the pope's authority does not extend to degrees prohibited by the divine law, which limitation is not made by writers who wish to diminish his authority, but accords with his own opinions. The cause alleged for the dispensation, the confirmation of peace, was insufficient, as there was already a firm peace. Another argument against the dispensation is the silence concerning the king's age, and the suggestion that he desired the marriage for the continuance of the treaty of peace, which was impossible at an age at which the common law does not admit discretion.

The brief which has since been produced is false, for many reasons. All persons must agree that the dispensation should be annulled.

It is expedient that the succession to the kingdom should be fixed and incontestable, and that the king's conscience should be quieted. The pope should grant his desires on account of his merits. (In the hand of Vannes)

Inigo di Mendoza to Charles V
London, 15 March 1529:

> [In cipher] Wolsey has sent to him to say that if the
> emperor please that the French king's mother and himself
> should meet him at Narbonne, he believes the pope would
> be very glad to join them there. Suspects these propositions
> are mainly put forward to stop the emperor's going to
> Italy.

Mai to Charles V
The pope has proposed of late to go to your majesty and to France, and moreover to send for the cardinal of England to help in a general peace, saying that the one will

have the office of St Peter, and the other that of St Paul. He has replied that he shall not object, provided there be no deceit, and that he will do his best to come to him. Since the pope's recovery, the matter has been talked of very warmly. For my part I never trust these things, and believe it to be a malicious invention to prevent the coming of the emperor. It was so that Pope Leo acted with the king of France, when it was said that he was going to Rome; he was on the road to Bologna, and agreed with him, and excused his going; and it appears that Pope Julius did the same. (Rome, 16 March 1529)

Clement VII to Wolsey

Notifies his convalescence, and thanks Wolsey for his kind compliments on the recovery of his health. (Rome, 18 March 1529)

Truce

Proclamation to be published by the sheriff of Yorkshire, declaring that the truce between the kings of England and France and the emperor will endure until two months after one of the princes gives notice of his intention to keep it no longer. (Richmond, 18 March 1529.)

Sanga to Campeggio

The English ambassadors have been with the pope, but not for long, owing to his debility. I need say nothing about the pope's inclination to satisfy the king with regard to his petitions, as the king and the cardinal must be aware of it. But the king's demands are such that the pope can come to no determination without taking counsel both from some of the cardinals and from learned persons, as he did on a former occasion when Dr Stephen Gardiner came to Orvieto. The pope cannot do this again, because the matters to be discussed are of such great importance that it would be necessary for him to take part in the whole of the discussion, which would compel him to remain five or six hours daily for several days with his counsellors, as he did on the previous occasion; and the pope's strength could not suffer so much fatigue without great danger to his health. The ambassadors themselves are witnesses to the pope's condition, and that he can do no more. I hope, however, that his Holiness will be able to attend to this matter in a few days. In the meanwhile no time shall be lost in obtaining the opinions of able and learned men as to the course which his Holiness may take to satisfy his majesty's desires. All that you write on this subject has been well considered. If he should be able to do nothing else, he will possibly cite the cause before himself. In short, the pope wishes to satisfy the king; but in a matter which might create so much scandal it is requisite that he should proceed cautiously, and find means to justify his proceedings. I know that your lordship, being anxious for the pope to take some resolution in this affair, and having expected a reply for so many days, would like to see the pope act differently; but I can say no more than I learn from his Holiness. The king and the cardinal have written to the pope, congratulating him on his recovery; to which letters a reply is made by the accompanying breves. Dr Stephen has presented other letters in the king's own hand and in that of the cardinal, touching their desire, etc. It will be necessary for the pope to reply in his own hand, but he cannot do so at present. (Rome, 19 March 1529)

Tuke to Wolsey

Received your letters this morning, and went straight to Greenwich. As the king had wrenched his foot, could not see him till eleven, when I delivered him the letters which have tarried so long. The king asked how you were, and whether your leg was mended. Told him it was only a little cold and friction. He then broke open Mr Stephen's letter, which is more full of desperation than that to your grace. Mr Bryan's is of the same tone, affirming that the pope would do nothing for the king, and adding "it might well be in his paternoster, but it was nothing in his creed". He spoke also of their coming to the pope's presence, etc. The king said there was little comfort in the letters, but I satisfied him as well as I could. He liked the clause deciphered that the registry of the brief could not be found, and so reserved his letters with one enclosed in Bryan's, directed to I know not whom, but I suppose to Mistress Anne. The Staplers will break up their household on 6th April next. (Greenwich, Palm Sunday evening, 21 March 1529)

Tuke to Wolsey

At 5 this morning letters arrived from Rome, Spain, France and Calais. The letters from Dr Stephen report little change in affairs. Mention is made of a great packet sent to the king, but I have only one little letter from Mr Stephen, one from Sir Francis Bryan and one from Mr Peter (Vannes), which I keep, to be delivered to the king as soon as he is ready. The others I have sent to you, and ordered Derby, who is at London, to repair to you, for deciphering those out of Spain. I will wait here all day, lest you should have anything to send me. Strange news is come from Calais, that the emperor is on board a fleet, attended by 12 ships, although the whole fleet amounts to more than six score, near Newport; but he would be compelled to disembark at Flushing. The deputy of Calais wrote to me, the day before, of a great fleet of Spaniards which passed by Calais. He thought they were a trade fleet. He has also heard the same news. The last letters from Spain mention that the emperor was going to Barcelona. As I get more news I will let you know. (Greenwich, Palm Sunday)

Vannes to Henry VIII

Will learn from their common letters what has taken place hitherto. By your majesty's command I visited the pope privately and found him very weak. I begged of him not to be offended with what I should say. He replied briefly that he was well aware of my good intentions. I told him what confidence your highness reposed in him; how long you had been expecting a favourable reply to your wishes; and the causes that moved you to desire a divorce. He expressed his anxiety to gratify the king. I told him what affection you had for him, how ready you were to make sacrifices in his behalf, and had always shown yourself ready so to do, when you expected nothing from him. He suddenly answered that he had submitted the examination of the brief (for on the disavowing of it Dr Stephen was very urgent) to Cardinal SS Quatuor; and when he has heard his opinion, he would do his best to satisfy the king. I replied that your majesty required his judgement on this matter as an indulgent father, and did not wish to be plunged into the technicalities of the law, which would be attended by so many delays and perilous consequences. I urged that everyone felt that the authority and benignity of the pope ought to be at hand as circumstances required, and that all men's feet were not to be fitted by the same slipper. I requested him not to deal in general replies, but by some definite response to gratify the expectations of your majesty; and if he had any fear of the emperor, to let me know it, and that he would determine at once upon the falsity of the brief. His Holiness replied that it would be best to produce the original as the best means of arriving at the truth. I answered that that would lend to long delays, and possibly to a repetition of the forgeries; that the presumptions of its spuriousness were manifold; and I offered to submit to the bishop of Verona the reasons collected by your majesty to prove its forgery. Considers this was a prudent course, for reasons subjoined.

I begged of him to let me have an answer which I might send to England. He told me he could give no certain answer as yet, but would agree to certain particulars. I asked him to be a little more explicit. I told him a fairer opportunity would not be wanting, if he had only the mind. He said he would summon SS Quatuor and Simonetta, and tell them how, for many reasons, he had resolved upon this business of the divorce to satisfy the king, and therefore they must find some honest means for doing it. I could get nothing else from him. I urged that your majesty was a much better, sincerer and more impartial friend than the emperor, if he had anything to hope or to fear. He said he feared nothing, but only wished a fair pretence to show to the emperor, and he could give no reason till he had consulted SS Quatuor. I told him I had searched all the registers carefully and could find nothing. The private registers we have not consulted, as they are often fraudulent. (Rome, 28 March 1529)

Tuke to Wolsey

Received your packet with letters from Rome, Spain and France. Read them to the king. In reading your grace's letter, his highness said, "This is of my lord cardinal's own hand." I said yea, which seemed very much to please him. He then asked for the letters in which mention was made of the cardinals and others favourable to the king's cause. I told him there was mention made of some in Mr Stephen's letters, but when I read him the letter he seemed to have expected more special advertisement of a great many his orators had made sure of, saying they were mentioned in letters written to him, which he went into his study and fetched, with one from the French king brought by De Langeais. I read him Mr Peter's letter and those of Spain.

He was not contented with the bishop of Worcester and Mr Almoner (Lee) for their delay in repairing to the emperor, as the emperor will learn the matter by the queen's servant, for whom and for Curzon he sent a safe-conduct, and not for the ambassadors.

He bade me read the devices of the bishop of Worcester, tending to throw suspicion on the brief to my lords of Norfolk, Suffolk and Rochford. I informed him that news had come that the emperor had ships in readiness in two places, for Rome and for Flanders, but of his going to Flanders I had heard no confirmation. He desired his ambassadors at Rome to secure for his cause as many cardinals as possible, as that would induce the pope to consent. I answered that they had been so instructed. Would have sent the letters sooner but was obliged to tarry all day, as Wolsey's letter was not deciphered. (London, this Monday at night)

APRIL 1529 TO MAY 1529

The pope proves to be as skilful at avoiding the pressures upon himself as Henry has been at applying them. However, he does seem to appreciate the significance, in terms of the future of the Church, of denying Henry that which he so clearly wishes.

Wm Poulet to Wolsey

Master treasurer of Wulsey and I proceed in your progress of Winchester, surveying the castles, manors, etc., for you to determine the dilapidations. The rate is over 200*l.*, besides the mills and weirs, little less than 200*l.* more. The

deer in the park are few; where you should have 1,000 you
have not 500. Certain hunters and fishers must be punished
for an example to others. We have taken care for the
goshawks, and I have warned all the townships to favour
the same. The expense to your predecessor was 5*l.* yearly. We
have respited the arrangement for an allowance to be made
by you to Wm Love, yeoman of your wardrobe in your
palace of Wulsey. We and Master Stokeley cannot induce
him to take less for his services than 10 marks. Your wardrobe
and staff are well kept, except two pieces of arras, injured
by the rats. Th. Polstede, your baily of Wargrave, is dead.
Your tenants are all well. On this day I begin my progress
again. On Monday I shall be at Taunton. (1 April 1529)

Erasmus to Cochlaeus

As to your doubt whether Henry VIII wrote the book and
two epistles against Luther which bear his name, many
entertain the same suspicion; and not without reason, since
it is looked upon as a prodigy, especially among the
Germans, that any prince should possess learning.
Although I would not assert that he received no assistance
in their composition, as others, even the most learned, do
on similar occasions, I am sure that he is both parent and
author of those things which go under his name. His father
was a man of the nicest judgement; his mother possessed
the soundest intellect and was remarkable for her prudence
as well as for her piety. When the king was no more than
a child, he was set to study. He had a vivid and active mind,
above measure able to execute whatever tasks he under-
took. He never attempted anything in which he did not
succeed. He had such natural dexterity that in the ordinary
accomplishments of riding and throwing the dart he out-
stripped every one. You would say that he was a universal
genius. In music he is no mean proficient. For mathemat-
ics he has shown remarkable docility. He has never

neglected his studies; and whenever he has leisure from his political occupations, he reads, or disputes—of which he is very fond—with remarkable courtesy and unruffled temper. You would say he is more of a companion than a king. For these little trials of wit he prepares himself by reading the schoolmen, Thomas, Scotus or Gabriel. I send you, as a specimen of his composition, a letter written entirely with his own hand when he was very young. When I had some doubts about it being his own composition, and Mountjoy failed to remove my doubts, he afterwards produced many letters of the king, with corrections three or four times repeated, all in the same hand. (Basle, 1 April 1529)

Campeggio to Sanga

During these holy days (Easter week) certain Lutheran books, in English, of an evil sort, have been circulated in the king's court. As yet I have been unable to obtain one, but I will endeavour to do so. I understand that by this book the Lutherans promise to abrogate all the heresies affecting the articles of the Faith, and to believe according to the divine law, provided that this king, with the most Christian king, will undertake to reduce the ecclesiastical state to the condition of the primitive Church, taking from it all its temporalities. I told the king that this was the devil dressed in angel's clothing, in order that he might the more easily deceive, and that their object was to seize the property of the Church; nor could any one promise the abrogation of so much heresy as now largely pervades the people. I represented that by councils and theologians it had been determined that the Church justly held her temporal goods. His majesty remarked that these Lutherans say that those decisions were arrived at by ecclesiastics, insinuating that now it is necessary for the laity to interpose. In reply I adduced various reasons, partly theological and partly temporal, telling him that this would be directly against his interests, for, as matters now stood, he obtained large sums of money; but if the laity had the goods of the Church this would no longer be the case, and they would probably grow rich and rebellious. The king also remarked that these men allege that the ecclesiastics, and especially the court of Rome, live very wickedly, and that we have erred in many things from the divine law. I replied that I would allow there were sins in Rome and in the court, because we are but men, but the Holy See had not deviated a jot from the true Faith. Finally, his majesty assured me of his good will, and that he had been and always would remain a good Christian, but that he had desired to communicate to me what had been told him by others; and if I wished to write to Rome, he was content, provided I did not state that I had heard it from his own mouth.

The Cardinal Wolsey was present, and after our departure thanked and commended me for my good offices. (London, 3 April 1529)

Mai to Charles V

Although the pope has had a relapse during Holy Week, I spoke to him on Thursday before yesterday, on which day the English ambassadors also had spoken to him, and afterwards the French.

The English ambassadors have lately pressed to get the dissolution of the marriage adjudged in England by the cardinal of York and Campeggio; and as they are half disappointed of that, they threaten with Luther and his sect. I treated this as a jest, and said that in such a case we should return the book to its author, which the king of England had written on this very subject, and strip him of the title of Defender of the Faith. This week I will make a request to the pope about it, according to your commandment, and his Holiness will not be sorry. All my study is to keep a close watch upon these ambassadors, which I think I do pretty sufficiently. It is four or five days since they had a meeting with lawyers, and I believe they have alleged nothing which has not been already answered. Takes counsel continually with the emperor's advocate on this matter. (Rome, 3 April 1529)

Ghinucci and Lee to Wolsey

On the 3rd of April the emperor sent a bishop and Inigo di Mendoza to accompany us to the court.

> [In cipher] He told us in Latin that the emperor was sorry that anything should happen to interfere with the ancient amities between England, Spain and Burgundy, and took heavily the intended divorce between the king and queen. About this he said many things that would have been better forborne, adjuring the king by the sacrament of matrimony, and by the obedience he owes to the Apostolic See, whose authority he pretended that the king seemed little to esteem. He declared the emperor's confidence in the pope and the Apostolic See, to which he said the emperor would appeal; but still he seemed to doubt the pope, for he spoke of appealing, if necessary, to a future council. He said also that the cause ought not to be determined in England, but at Rome, and that the king must have patience if the emperor defend the queen in her right. Hope to send this more extended by their next. Mgr Pernott, then, to declare the validity of the marriage and the injustice of the king's cause, produced the brief, declaring that the emperor, in order that the truth might be known, would send to the king a transumpt under the authority of three bishops, but he would not send the original, for fear of miscarriage.
>
> To this they answered that many things might have been forborne, especially the adjuration of the king by the

sacrament of matrimony, concerning which it was
notorious that the king held the Christian and Catholic
opinion, and had no such sinister intentions as to need
adjuration by the sacrament. His reverence and obedience
to the Apostolic See has always been apparent, and he has
done nothing but what he can justify to God and the
world. He has as humbly submitted his cause to the pope
as any private man of the poorest sort would have done,
and in this he had anticipated the emperor, who need not
labour to bring the cause to the knowledge of the pope. It
was useless to send the transumpt, for the brief itself was
required as that on which both the king and queen
consider the validity of the matrimony to hang, and it was
only reasonable that it should be in their custody.

After this the emperor spoke to them apart, saying that
all this was done to get justice for the queen; and he
endeavoured to justify himself.

Henry VIII to Gardiner and his colleagues

Charges them to use all diligence in declaring the king's
cause to the pope, in which he trusts they will find great
help from the good advice and address of the bishop of
Verona (Salviati). If they cannot be admitted to the pope's
presence, they may signify to the bishop the king's whole
mind. He will be able to counteract the malice of the archbishop of Capua, who is thought to be one of the chief
authors of the falsities, crafts and abuses set forward to hinder the king's cause. He is, therefore, especially to be
entertained; but they must gain as many other friends as
possible.

Wishes to know what advocates they have on their
side. Desires them to retain some notable and excellent
divine, a friar or other, who will firmly stick to that *quod
pontifex ex jure divino non potest dispensare* etc. (Signed at the
commencement. Greenwich, 6 April 1529)

Stephen Gardiner to Henry VIII

Though they have done the best they could to obtain from the pope the accomplishment of the king's desires, they have not prevailed, but now see it called in question whether the authority given to the legates shall be revoked. What has been done will be found in their common letters to Wolsey. Hopes the king will accept his good will in good part. Is sorry to see his highness's cause so handled. The king has not been handled according to his merits by the pope or some other; it becomes not Gardiner to arrect the blame certainly to any man, and the pope shows Campeggio's letters for his discharge. The king can judge of this better than he can write. Wishes to know what to do further.

The pope is content to grant the bulls,* saving in that matter, *de animadversione in clericos*, about which he would consult with Cardinal SS Quatuor. He wishes he could grant as easily the other petitions, which he knows the king has more at heart, adding, by and by, that he would, for the wealth of Christendom, the queen were in her grave; and, as he thought, the emperor would be thereof most glad of all; saying also that he thought, like as the emperor hath destroyed the temporalities of the Church, so shall she be the cause of the destruction of the spiritualities; making exclamation of his misfortune in whose person these two adversities should chance, and upon the occasion of that family.

When they speak with him, think they will have all things, but in the end his council deny all, because Cardinal SS Quatuor has been sick, and is every other day sickly. Usually when the cardinal is whole, the pope is sick. (Rome, 4 May 1529)

---

* Giving the pope's consent for the dissolution of corrupt monasteries in England.

Francis Bryan to Henry VIII

Since my last of the 21st, we have, according to your commandment by Alysaunder, opened all to the pope, first by
fair means and then by foul; but neither fair nor foul will
serve, as you will see by our letter to the cardinal. You will
see by our common letters, a copy of which we send, in
what situation we are. Master Stephen, in the presence of
the pope, so answered for your grace that he made the
pope ashamed of his own deeds, who would have excused
the cause as best he could. As for what you write to us, that
Campeggio is your servant, and will do what he can for
you, these are fair words only because he wishes to have
the bishopric of Durham. He has written here to the pope
to say that neither he nor Francis Campanys ever made any
special promise to your grace, but in general words, and he
bids the pope trust to it, as the pope might be sure of him.
Whatever they tell you the pope will do for you is "the
glose and not the text". This is true, for the pope showed
the letter to Master Stephen and Master Peter (Vannes). If
the cardinal feels aggrieved, or any other, let him kick; for
I do it not of malice, but according to my duty. I could tell
you more of my mind in an hour's talking than I could
write in a week, and shall be glad to come home, as I can
do you here no service. I dare not write unto my cousin
Anne the truth of this matter, because I do not know your
grace's pleasure whether I shall so do or no; wherefore, if
she be angry with me, I most humbly desire your grace to
make mine excuse. I have referred to her in her letter all
the news to your grace, so your grace may use her in this
as ye shall think best. (Rome, 5 May 1529)

Wolsey to Gardiner, Bryan, Casale and Vannes

The king has received your letters by Thaddeus, and I have
received yours of the 28th and 29th March and of the 8th,
19th, 20th and 21st of April to myself, concerning your

conferences, and thank you for your service and dexterity. The king, although your desires have not taken effect, received your services with thankfulness, and does not attribute to you any blame. He perceives that whatever solicitations have been made to the pope for the further- ance of his cause depend entirely upon the emperor's will, whom the pope dare not oppose. The emperor, as appears by sundry letters, has interposed his power unfavourably to the king. The king, finding the pope's ingratitude, is resolved to dissemble with him, and to proceed here on his cause by virtue of the commission granted to me and Campeggio. He is resolved to revoke all his ambassadors except Sir Gregory. Therefore, Gardiner and Bryan are to return; and had it not been for Gardiner's absence, whose services are so much required, he would have commenced his process before this Whitsuntide. You are to obtain, as best you can, the amplification of the commission, using all possible dexterity, advertising the pope how sorry the king is that whereas he expected to find in him a fast and lov- ing friend, he studies more to please the emperor, who is the common enemy of Christendom, than the king; which is not the way to preserve friendship. Still, as the king is willing to trust him to the utmost, he hopes that the pope will prove the love he has always professed for him, and declare by his acts the uttermost of his intent and disposi- tions that you, Gardiner and Bryan, may not return empty-handed. You shall also urge the grief of myself and Campeggio in being thus disappointed, entreating the pope as from myself to weight well the great exigencies of the case. Leaving everything else, your whole efforts are to return to the security and amplification which you have transmitted, with notes in the margin showing where it is ineffectual, desiring you to get it devised anew and regranted with additions; telling the pope that it was so much defaced and injured by wet and carriage as that it is detained by him to whom you directed it, and you are likely to be blamed afresh, according to the best of your remembrance, inserting "other pregnant, fat and available words as is possible".

I advertise you that the king has received fresh letters out of Spain in answer to those sent by Curzon for exhibition of the original breve. The letters are of sundry dates, the last of the 21st of April, when the emperor was at Saragossa. He wishes to make a demonstration of his coming to Italy, but we hear that he is wholly unprepared. He is endeavouring to sow dissension between this court and France; but you may tell the pope he will not succeed, and that the French king is resolved on war with the emperor, and he will be assisted by a body of men under the duke of Suffolk, who is now sent to France. This may possibly shake his confidence in the emperor. The emperor refuses to send the brief to England, but makes show of sending it to Rome, as he would have the cause decided there. I send you a copy of it, with some remarks indicating the manifest proof of forgery, especially in reference to the dates. This matter will require secrecy.

The king hears that the emperor's ambassador has an authentic copy of the brief, and that on the proof of any falsity the original might be altered and a new one forged; he desires them therefore to dissemble their knowledge of the error in the date, and to endeavour, whither by the pope, or some other secret means, to get a sight of the copy, and to get an authentic copy made, which Gardiner and Bryan shall bring over with them. This would prevent the alteration of the original, or a new forgery. Gardiner and Bryan are to bring with them everything they have obtained. Vannes will remain till their arrival in England, that he also may have a colour to desire the pope not to let him return *vacuis minibus*.

Meantime Vannes and Casale must take special care to prevent the advocation of the cause, the revocation of the commission, inhibition, recusation or any other act that may delay proceedings here. They must consult the lawyers they have retained about the invalidation of the brief, putting the proofs thereof in an authentic form. The emperor, knowing that the king is trying to prove the falsity of the brief, will probably, relying upon the pope's friendship, send it to Rome, to have the matter decided there, by having a transumpt made by the pope or other person by his command, and thus prevent the legates from giving sentence. They must look out for this, and tell the pope that although he has refused to decree the brief false, the English ambassadors will not consent to such a transumpt, but will protest accordingly, by means of an authentic instrument.

Wishes Gardiner and Bryan to bring back with them the bulls and expeditions for the king's colleges and his, unless obtaining them would cause much delay.

Mai to Charles V

The English ambassadors press the pope hard to declare the brief a forgery, and his Holiness has signified to me his desire that the protest should be made. Is informed, both by the archbishop of Capua, Salviati, and by cardinals Tortosa, S Crucis and Caesarinus that the pope had said to them that the English were incessantly coming upon the subject, and that it was needful to stand with averted eyes.

I have drawn up the protest and communicated it to Andrea del Burgo, but I have omitted something of what was put in it, in order not to irritate the king of England to the prejudice of the queen. Nevertheless, I have taken care not to annoy the pope more. I desired the pope to give me a notary of the chamber. He said if I would let him choose one, he would comply, but he was afraid of what others would say. Afterwards he sent to me to say he thought better not to give me one, but that I should apply to the chamberlain. The same day he sent to me by Sanga to say that it was better the protest should not be made to him, except when he should be in *signatura*, and the party present.

I was afraid they would delay the *signatura*, as they had already delayed it three or four months, and said I could not wait, for two causes, viz., because a messenger was about to leave and I required to inform the emperor. Moreover, Andrea del Burgo's concurrence was required and he had not recovered from his gout; and as to the notary, if his Holiness did not think it right to give me one, as he had promised, I would find one for myself, as I only desired that he should be a notary of the chamber, out of respect to his Holiness. Another day Sanga returned, and said the pope was content that I should do it whenever I pleased, and wished to know what the protest contained. I accordingly read it to him, word for word, and he quite approved of it. That same day Andrea del Burgo was at the palace, and arranged to be with the pope in the morning. At last we went there together, along with many Spaniards, when the pope told us he was obliged to give us rather a harsh answer, but that need not trouble us until we had published the protest. Seeing what he was driving at, I said to him, "Holy Father, we will do so; help us with justice that we may be able to help ourselves." And thereupon entered Alonzo de Cuevas as notary, and Marradas and Jacobo Salviati as witnesses, and the act was made as your majesty will see.

The same day I found two spies in the palace after dinner, and I learned that the ambassadors of England had come and held an interview with the pope, from which they came away very angry and bullying.

The other day the pope told me that they used a threatening tone, saying that if the queen did not consider

England a safe place, as little did they hold Rome and the pope to be safe, on account of your army. I said their wisdom was apparent, when on one side they threatened, and on the other said that we were not secure; and as for what touched his Holiness, they had told him sufficiently often that they wanted him to remove to Avignon, and that but for the pope's wisdom they would have made him commit every day a thousand errors. The pope said to me he would have a *signatura* another day, and he sent to me to say that I should intimate the *signatura* and the commission to the English ambassadors and give them a copy of the commission. I answered that I did not want anything with the English ambassadors or with the king, but that his Holiness should revoke his cause, and that he might, if he pleased, order the dean of the referendaries to intimate it to them and to me. They afterwards told me that it was customary to intimate the *signaturas* and commission; and I did so, not to raise needless obstacles.

Relates communications with the referendaries, and of Andrea del Burgo with the cardinal of Ancona. Mentions having discovered that the English ambassadors had given a very rich fur to the cardinal of Ravenna, who is the nephew of Ancona, and had sent a messenger to the latter before he came to Rome. In the morning, fearing that the English ambassadors would come to the *signatura*, went to mass at St Peter's, and sent to see if they were coming. Having learnt that they had come, and the ambassador of France along with them, and that they had sent from the palace for the ambassador of Venice, complained to Sanga that the politics of the League were allowed a place in matters of justice. Sanga said they too had accused the pope of partiality, and it was no wonder they were jealous. At last they would not come, either having received some admonition from Sanga, or being disappointed that I was there.

Some time afterwards Simonetta came to me, and said the English wanted to speak to the pope in full consistory and in my presence, if I wished to be there. I said I had nothing to do with them, but that the servants of your majesty refused nothing of this kind, and we entered and saluted with sufficient courtesy. The pope then desired us to say what it was we wanted. I said we had been told that the English wished to speak in my presence, and that I had come to hear them. Their lawyer ambassador then said in Latin that late yesterday one who said he represented the pope had very improperly cited them with so little warning that they had not consulted upon the matter, and had no power as regards this article; that they had received a copy of the commission, in which were passages that touched the honour of the king their master, because they say that he wished to have a divorce from the queen, although his Holiness knew well that this did not proceed from the king's own desire, but from the scruples of his conscience; that the pope knew very well he, the speaker, was the first that came hither to his Holiness, and had asked him for counsel in this matter on the king's behalf, in the presence of SS Quatuor and Monte; and that if the pope had thought right he might have undeceived them, and said that there was no reason to pursue it further, but that he never would give them any advice, and this he protested another time before the same persons; all that he obtained from the pope was the commission, and, since he had given it, he could not revoke it without injury to the king. At this the pope was much disturbed, all the more because the English ambassador said two or three times, "This I say, that the Imperial ambassador may know it, and may not suppose that my king is such a one as would seek a divorce."

To this I replied simply, "It is well that everything should be known"—adding no more, not to disturb his argument.

Moreover, he said he did not know why we Spaniards should be more interested in Henry's kingdom and his daughter then they were, that his daughter was very dear to the king and to all the people, and that she takes care to do no wrong; and that the brief which was produced was false, though he did not know who had forged it—only all the lawyers held it false, and his Holiness ought so to judge it.

In reply Mai said that if the messenger had done his duty badly, he hoped his Holiness would have him punished; that it was true he had sent him to comply with the custom of this court, which was better than they did at Orvieto when they cited the ministers of the emperor; that their allegation that they had no powers was incredible, they being such honoured ambassadors of so wise a king; that at the time they left England they knew that Muscetula had made application for this, which we now petition for, and that now they came into this cause requesting his Holiness to declare the brief false without hearing the party or seeing the brief, which is in Spain; and that they cannot be procurators for one article in the cause, and not for another; and if this were the state of matters there would be no necessity for a procurator at all, for as the commission had been given to Campeggio without our knowledge, it might be revoked without theirs. I disclaimed having uttered any injurious words of the king, whom I had always spoken of with great honour. To be divorced was to be separated, and I could not understand it otherwise; and whether it was of his own motion or by the counsel of others, I did not know. I only knew the meaning of the word. We were very glad to hear the king treated his daughter well, whom I called princess, and hoped they would every day treat her better. As to the treatment of the queen, his Holiness knew it; and that if Campeggio were on our side, *no se consintio,* as appears by the protest made by Muscetula, which I produced anew; besides this there were innumerable new causes for revoking it.

The English ambassador replied again, and I rejoined.

I knew that the pope was very much provoked by the English, and that he has said a certain word in our favour, although he has ordered, under pain of excommunication, that no one repeat it.

He has put the matter off to another *signatura*. I will continue to do my best with these referendaries, and I think it a good sign that these English ambassadors have spoken at such length, as it is evident they wish to lay the blame upon the pope, and discharge themselves before us and the world, fearing that they will not succeed. As to the suggestion about poison, I did not think it proper to reply, as the words were general, and might be interpreted otherwise. Moreover, it was not desirable to irritate them against the queen.

The archbishop of Capua is afraid that the cardinal of Ravenna may be drawn over to the English side by English money.

Has heard that the pope has given the English ambassadors a brief that the emperor should send hither within a certain time the brief in question, to ascertain its genuineness, or that he should send it into England, otherwise they would proceed in the cause; yet I understand the English are not satisfied with it. Since the above took place, the pope has been ill and has given Andrea del Burgo and myself to understand that the English are very much provoked at us, and have written a thousand follies into England, especially that the king should marry whom he pleased without waiting for more declarations, and suggesting that they should turn away the queen from there; and with this his Holiness begs that we should not press the revocation of the cause at present, but I have insisted upon it on the ground of justice, and I do not intend to desist.

I have just received an allegation of what the English ambassadors have objected to this revocation. Have not time to send a copy. I fear the weakness of the pope more than anything. (Rome, 9 May 1529)

Mai to Charles V

The pope has frequent relapses, and latterly from an affront given him by the English ambassadors—of which I have written apart to your majesty, not to mix up one thing with another. Latterly he has been made so ill that we have been in great fear for him. He has since been rather better, but many don't believe that he is safe, and his physician told me yesterday that if he have another relapse his case is desperate. I have been informed on good authority that his Holiness has an oil which has been very efficacious against poison; the physicians greatly disapprove of its use, but he keeps it without their known. (Rome, 11 May 1529)

Campeggio to Salviati

With your letters of 19th March there came no letters for this king or the cardinal of York from their ambassadors, at which they were greatly astonished. They did not receive any till the 6th inst., when some were brought by Thaddeus. You wrote that the matter should be discussed within a few days, and that the pope would be present; but I have heard no more from you; nor am I enlightened by the two letters of the 11th and 15th of April from my brother, Mgr di Feltro. Pray consider to how much displeasure and confusion I am subjected on this account. They (the king and Wolsey) can hardly believe that I have received no reply to all the points of my letter. They tell me that in fact they can hope for nothing from the pope, and that his Holiness refers all things to us (the legates).

This king and the cardinal of York have letters from Spain, of 21st and 23rd April, from the auditor of the chamber (Ghinucci) and from their ambassador (Lee), certifying them that the brief is false. They, therefore, argue that they have no guarantee or assurance that the bull is valid; and they insist that the trial shall proceed and the cause be dispatched. I have replied that I am content, and will not fail to do my duty. I believe they will proceed with all diligence after this feast of Whitsuntide, especially as the said persons write from Spain that the emperor and those of the court regard it as a settled thing that the cause will be cited by us and brought into court.

When they said that nothing was to be hoped for from the pope, they added that the pope was in agreement with the emperor, and would do nothing without his permission; that the pope wished to go to Spain if the emperor was content, and would proclaim a truce if it was agreeable to the emperor; and that the pope had respect to the emperor in this matrimonial cause. I replied that I was not aware of any agreement between the pope and the emperor, and could not believe that the pope was bound by any agreement to give offence or be adverse to the king. With regard to the matrimonial cause, I said I knew for certain that the pope was exceedingly well disposed towards the king, and that his respect for the emperor would not cause him to deviate a jot from that which he could justly do in his favour, as he desired to do him every service, provided it lay in his power; but that they ought to consider that this matter touched one of the sacraments of the Church and might create great scandal, so that the pope was constrained to proceed very deliberately and could do nothing inconsistent with justice, as I had frequently been told by him in various conversations on this subject.

York, however, told me that their ambassadors did not despair of being able to obtain something from the pope;

but the king, on Sunday the 9th, told me that he intended to dispatch Thaddeus thither immediately, with orders for Bryan and Dr Stephen (Gardiner) to return, and that the auditor of the chamber (Ghinucci) would return to Italy and would be his ambassador there together with the cavalier Casale. The king then added (in Latin), "I do not importune the pope for the creation of cardinal, like other kings, but, in behalf of the said auditor, I certainly wish he would create him cardinal at my request." The king manifested very great desire for this, and said many things in praise of the auditor.

York has told me that the emperor is urging three things upon them: a particular peace between them; if they refuse the first, a suspension of arms; or else a particular truce. They have refused the first two, but would consent to the third, with the inclusion of the French king. The cardinal added that the emperor is doing his utmost to separate them from the French king, or the French king from them, because they are informed that an agreement is being negotiated with the French king by means of Madame Eleanor, sister of the emperor, and that she has recently sent a Portuguese to the French court. Henry and Wolsey had determined to send Master Russell, of the king's chamber, to the French king, but have since changed their mind, and they now send the duke of Suffolk, the king's kinsman, and Master Fitzwilliam, treasurer of the king's household, who is, I understand, a noble person, of great valour and skilled in the art of war. They send them in order that they may be in counsel with the French king and have authority and means to give him assistance, when they have made sure that the French king will do his duty, and take good order for conducting the war vigorously. York told me, as a secret, that they intend to give him (Francis) a large band of English. It seems that they propose, if the emperor goes into Italy, that the French king shall enter it also. But I believe that when they have obtained a settlement of this matrimonial cause, which they consider as binding them to the French king's girdle, they will be ready to accept an agreement with the emperor. Wolsey has said to me many times (in Latin), "On the dissolution of this marriage we shall easily find some means of agreeing with the emperor, and there will be no more clamours." They propose, in the first place, to content the queen, leaving her the rank which she now holds, and all that she chooses to demand, except the king's person; and next to satisfy the emperor by making a new marital alliance between the emperor's natural daughter and this king's natural son.

Some days ago certain persons of account passed from Spain to Flanders to hold a diet there on the 10th inst. and to demand in the emperor's name 15,000 foot in pay for Italy, and 500 of their men-at-arms. I believe they will obtain a large subsidy.

The cardinal and the king have received the briefs enclosed in yours of 19th March. I made an excuse for there being no answer to their letters in the pope's hand, on account of his Holiness's indisposition. For the last five months I have sustained very heavy expenses, without receiving any remittances. I have been subjected to great displeasure, and know not how long it will last. (London, 12 May 1529)

Campeggio to Salviati

The cardinal of York by letter ordered my secretary to repair to him immediately, with Francesco and Darius, and to be at Windsor before night, as he had something of importance to tell them. And this was owing to the arrival of the cavalier Casale. They reached Windsor at sunset, and found Wolsey at table. The cardinal had been with the king all the day, and caused them to be told that as he was fatigued they were to return in the morning at nine o'clock. They did so, and presented themselves yesterday morning (the 19th) to Wolsey as he issued from his chamber. Wolsey said nothing to them, but conducted them to the king; and after he had first spoken with the king, he sent to call them, that is Francesco and my secretary. Then the cardinal drew aside, and left the king to speak to them.

Turning to Francesco the king said, "Do you not remember that the first time you spoke to me you told me that his Holiness would do for me all he could, *etiam de plenitudine potestatis*, and that the Rev. Campeggio told me the same?" He then recalled the place where they met, and the circumstances which then took place. Francesco replied, "Most serene king, I remember the place and the time, and the substance of all that I announced to your majesty in our lord's name, especially that he would do all he could . . . but I do not recollect using the form of words specified, or that the Rev. Campeggio made use of them."

While they were disputing the point the cardinal interposed, as if to assist them in recalling those words to memory, and said to Francesco, "Do you not remember that, when it was said that his Holiness would do for my king all that lay in his power, it was questioned what this power was, if he could use it with justice, and with authority and power; and that the answer was that he would not fail in anything that was possible?" The cardinal wished to infer that, if the promise of all that the pope could do includes *plenitudinem potestatis*, this last was necessarily due to them.

To this Francesco replied, "Whether these words involve this *plenitudo* or not, or whether this may be argued from that, I will not now dispute. I know very well that the words specified were not in my commission, and could not be, for when I departed from his Holiness this point was not in discussion."

The king then said, "Upon this promise *de plenitudine* I despatched Dr Stephen Gardiner, by whom I have demanded from his Holiness a thing which his own representatives even confess that he can grant *de plenitudine*, but he is unwilling to concede it; and when he is urged to observe what he has promised, he says that neither himself nor his representatives have promised it. And upon this point he has showed to my said ambassadors a letter of the Rev. Campeggio, in which he writes that neither he nor M Francesco has promised any such things, but that they have always spoken in general terms, and uttered words without any meaning etc.; and the English ambassadors declare and assert that they write the exact words, though in English." And here the king, and still more the cardinal, made a great complaint, and said that they are not to be treated with words or in general terms, and that such terms ought not to be used with a king, or between friends. Francesco replied in an appropriate manner, and then my secretary denied that I had promised the *plenitudo*, or written as above.

They then produced the letters of Dr Stephen, and wished to recite the very words which the ambassadors had read in my letter, but they were in English. It was represented that no argument could be founded upon them, because it was very likely that our letters had been misinterpreted, and that here the ambassadors' letters might be misunderstood, as we were more interested in the matter than they. They then complained that we had not gone beyond these general terms, and said that if their ambassadors had made no opposition you would by this time have revoked the cause from here, and thus have laid a great burden on the cardinal of York and me, and a great outrage on the king. And here the cardinal dilated at length, lamenting that the pope took such little account of the king and of the kingdom, and less of himself and his life; but he said he would never desert this cause, and would do and say before all princes that which Francesco will more fittingly declare by word of mouth.

As the cardinal was doing his utmost to excite enmity, my secretary finally made answer to so many complaints and menaces thus:

> Most serene king and most reverend lordship, you ought to consider that my most reverend master is resident here with you as a legate of the Apostolic See, as a cardinal, as a judge, and as the servant and friend of your majesty and reverend lordship, and that by no words or reasons he can be diverted from doing the office of a legate, a good cardinal, a judge, and of your friend and servant; and in all these points he will ever regard and prefer that argument and that cause which may justly be preferred above all others. If his Holiness does not comply with your majesty's desires, he excuses himself because he cannot do so with justice, and because it would be to the prejudice of a third party.

They replied that their demands were prejudicial to no person whatever. Lastly, as Francesco and the secretary were departing, the king said to them both in Latin, "Be good friends to me, and have pity on me."

They afterwards spoke with the cardinal apart. Francesco will relate all that passed at greater length. They have asked him to stay a short time longer, but as I am to go to Richmond tomorrow with the cardinal of York, I will endeavour to obtain leave for him to depart. If I am unable to do so, this letter will be brought by Silvester Darius, whom they have dismissed.

With regard to my letters, the English ambassadors at Rome write that you had refused to show them, and that they had read in them that the king and Wolsey exaggerate every slightest word. Pray, consider where I am, and in what an odious negotiation, and how much inconvenience and damage this mode of proceeding may cause me. Owing to this I am subject to so much displeasure and trouble that I can say no more. (London, 20 May 1529)

Wolsey to Gardiner, Bryan, Gregory Casale and Peter Vannes
I have received your letters of the 4th by the hands of Alexander, and the king has received his, by which we learn that the king is frustrated of his expectations from the pope, your despair to obtain any favours from him, and the strange treatment in calling upon you to answer why the supplication presented by the Imperial ambassador for advocation of the cause should not proceed. I ascertained by Thaddeus, who I trust has arrived long before, that, avoiding all other projects, you are to apply for a new commission, and that Stephen and Bryan are to return home; but as it seems that there is no hope of obtaining such a commission, and Stephen and Bryan are on the way home, the king sends this bearer, Mr Bennet, well learned in the laws, to oppose the Imperialists. He will signify to you what you are to do, ascertaining you that, failing all your requests, you are to represent to the pope the danger of losing the king's favour. Seeing, however, that the pope would gladly preserve the king's favour, you are not to be rigorous, but only to look what may be done touching the protestation which you will learn from Bennet's instructions. You are to withstand all the importunity of the Imperialists for revoking the commission given to Campeggio and myself, which would not fail to irritate the king and the nobles, and withdraw them from their obedience to the See Apostolic. As it appears from your last letters that the commission was not wholly denied, but that you were ordered to confer with the cardinals Anconitane and Simonetta upon the same, and it is possible that more fat, pregnant and effectual clauses may yet be

obtained, it is the king's pleasure that if Gardiner and Bryan have not yet left, they shall still endeavour to see what can be done in this matter, taking care not to alienate the pope, or induce him to incline to an avocation of the cause. You shall further dissuade the pope from sending to Spain for the original brief, and, if the nuncio has gone for that purpose, obtain a commandment from the pope that no mention be made of it, for which you can find very good excuse.

It appears by certain letters to the king and myself that the pope is desirous of finding a way of satisfying the king, but, after consulting the lawyers, can find no satisfactory means. If, therefore, the pope proposes an avocation of the cause, you shall tell him this is not the way to please the king, and conduct yourselves accordingly. (Richmond, 21 May 1529)

Du Bellay to —

I assure you, Wolsey is in the greatest pain he ever was. The dukes of Suffolk and Norfolk, and the others, lead the king to believe that he has not done as much as he could have done to promote the marriage. Francis and Madame could not do him a greater favour than to let Suffolk and his friend know by good means how urgently he has pressed them hitherto to take the thing in hand. By their last letters from Rome they feel less assurance than they had, so they are sending back Dr Bennet in post, praying, entreating, threatening, etc. I know that the pope has a greater mind than they suppose to revoke their commission. They wanted him at once to declare the enlarged brief null and void; which he would not do. This is one of the knotty points of the business. They expect that the matter once commenced will only last two months, but I promise you it will last more than four. Moreover, before the execution of peace there might occur the death of the queen of

England, or of her daughter, which would put an end to all enmities on their side. Wolsey has spoken to Campeggio of our matter of peace, which the latter has reported to me. I made light of it, and spoke of a universal peace. I think he will intimate this to your Salviati. They have power from the pope. If anything be done here, depend upon it they want to put their pin in the game. Mark the words of the treaty of perpetual peace, that you can do nothing without the advice and consent of England; but if anything good be done you can, I think, say that it is with his advice and consent, seeing that he himself made and signed the articles, and pressed their being proposed, even to threats. So that he has no cause to complain if they are accepted by the emperor. In that case also you have the duke of Suffolk and Wolsey's son in your hands. I am sure that if, without making appearance of anything, you show Suffolk my letters, you will do great pleasure to Wolsey. (London, 22 May 1529)

Campeggio to Salviati

Last evening I arrived here at Richmond and learned that the cardinal had dispatched a courier to Rome with Dr Bennet, who was formerly destined to go as ambassador with Dr Knight, but they returned on the arrival of Dr Stephen Gardiner, who is now recalled, and this man is sent in his stead, in order that he may attend to their affairs. Do not be surprised if on their arrival you have not received my letters, because I was not aware of their departure.

I have found York greatly exasperated at the citation made to the ambassadors of this king, as he does not understand the custom of the papal court, and to him the thing seems very strange. But when he learned from me how judicial matters are conducted in Rome, he became pacified, as also with respect to the refusal to revoke the

brief. I gave him to understand that the pope had not satisfied this their desire, because he could not do so with
justice, or without the greatest scandal. They rest contented
with this explanation. The cardinal told me that, in consequence of what I had frequently said to him, they had
represented to the king that that demand was not honourable, and could not be granted, but his majesty insisted
that it should be attempted.

I now find his lordship, and the king by his report, to
be in great suspense, owing to this citation. I think they
have begun to suspect, from what their ambassadors have
written to them, that I had solicited this; and on this
account they make use of great menaces, as you will more
fully understand from M Francesco, the bearer. Wolsey
inquired whether I credited such a revocation, and said to
me that the pope was well acquainted with the cause, the
parties between whom it depended, the parties to whom
it was entrusted and the place where it was to be tried; that
besides all this, he had promised not to revoke it from
England, but to confirm the sentence of the legates; that
his Holiness had revoked it because he wished to please
the emperor, and would by this means destroy the king, the
kingdom and his lordship; and that they would not toler-
ate it. But they cannot on any account persuade themselves
that it is true the pope intends to revoke it. I commit
myself to the most sage judgement of the pope, who will
doubtless take the best and least scandalous course. I
believe they will write warmly to the French king on this
subject.

Sanga to Campeggio

My last letter was dated the 15th inst., when I had received
yours of 3rd April, the duplicate of which, with a short
postscript, came with your letter of the 12th. I see that up
to that date my letter of 19th March was the last you had

received; so that you still have to answer mine of the 10th, 13th and 27th April, and of the 1st, 4th, 8th and 15th May. I should be displeased that none of these letters had reached you on the 12th, if I did not learn from your letter to the bishop of Feltre that the cause of the delay was that the courier had forwarded them to the court of France in the packet for the Cardinal Salviati, my son. I informed you of the protestations made here, and of the commissions presented by the ambassadors of the emperor and the king of Hungary, of which I sent copies, stating that the pope had till then refused to sign them, and that he wished to do everything consistent with justice for the king's satisfaction. Since then the pope has had a fourth attack of his complaint, and has been taking the water of the grotto of Viterbo, so that little negotiation has been carried on. I cannot therefore tell you any more about that cause than I have already written. Signor Bryan and Doctor Stephen Gardiner are about to depart.

To yours of 3rd April I made answer on the 21st ult. It only remains to reply to the postscript added to the duplicate, touching the Lutheran books dispersed throughout the court. The pope was greatly pleased with what you said in conversing with the king on this subject, and also with the good mind showed by the king. Although the king is moved to this by his virtue, and may expect worthy rewards for it from God, you are to thank him infinitely on the pope's behalf, and pray him firmly to maintain that shield of defence of the Church which he took up with so much glory to himself. You are also to thank the most illustrious cardinal of York, whose vigilance and prudence, combined with the king's good mind, has kept and keeps that island clear of such monsters. This result appears miraculous, considering how many times attempts have been made to introduce the king to write, as he did on a former occasion, something worthy of his majesty; he would renew the glory he has already acquired, and it would for a long while assure that most happy kingdom from such contagion.

Would to God that, either by means of the king and cardinal, or by some other, a way to some peace could be found, as otherwise everything will go to ruin. I think there could not be much to arrange if the envoys of Madame Margaret and the duke of Savoy bring back a favourable reply from Spain. By letters of the 26th ult. we learn that these envoys had been despatched by the emperor. We have heard no more touching his majesty's coming.

In order that you should have some "entertainment" while it is being decided how to satisfy your pensions for the legation and for the (office of the) *signatura*, an assignment of 1,000 scudi has been given to the bishop of Feltre, who will endeavour that you shall be able to avail yourself of it. You know the pope's poverty, and that we have exhausted all we had. Do not therefore be surprised that you have not been provided betimes or to the full amount due.

Although everything has been done to let these ambassadors know that the pope has done nothing for the king's satisfaction, because he could not act contrary to duty without very great scandal, yet I doubt whether they, being very zealous in their master's service, will rest satisfied. It is needful that you should take the utmost precautions that any complaint they make on their arrival may not infuse dissatisfaction with his Holiness into the mind of the king and cardinal, as he is doing what he can to satisfy the king, provided he see a way to do so without very great scandal.

There will have, by way of Germany, fresher advices than we have of the preparations and movements of the Turk. Here we have letters from Venice of the 22nd,

stating that he was to march in person on the 2nd, and that
no sultan ever made greater preparation for war than this
one. I foresee ruin, unless God help us. King Ferdinand, by
his ambassador here, has prayed for assistance. As it is the
common cause of Christendom, the pope would have
liked to do more; but as he could give nothing else he has
given him the same faculties of aiding himself by imposts
on ecclesiastical property as were given to the last king.
This enemy is one to be dreaded, especially as he finds the
body of Christendom weak and bloodless, and Germany
divided. (Rome, 29 May 1529)

[In cipher] If the pope were not certain that you are
strictly mindful of the injunctions which he gave you
by word of mouth, and which have been since written
to you many times, especially in the first four letters
which I wrote when you first entered into England,
and lastly by Francesco da Colle, he would be in a
very anxious state of mind, and would have expected to
have been informed by yours of the 12th that the cause
would be proceeded with after Whitsuntide. His
Holiness has always desired that it should be protracted,
in order to find some means by which he could satisfy
the king without proceeding to the sentence. You may
rest assured that the citation of the cause hither, which
you have frequently insisted on, has been deferred, not
because it was doubted whether the matter could be
treated with less scandal here than there, but because his
Holiness has ever shrunk from having to take a step
which would offend the mind of that most serene king.
But since you have not been able to prevent the
commencement of the proceedings, his Holiness warns
you that the process must be slow, and that no sentence
must in any manner be pronounced. For this purpose
you will not lack a thousand means and pretexts, if

upon no other point, at least upon the breve which has been produced.

You have sustained this burden until now with great dexterity and patience, and therefore the pope doubts not you will in like manner be able to sustain it till such time as your counsel to cite the cause hither can be followed with less offence to the king's mind. That course cannot justly be objected to, as the Imperial and the Hungarian ambassadors have made protests and presented their commissions, of which I sent you copies. But his Holiness has continued to shirk signing them, by holding out the hope to them that no proceedings will be taken there unless the commissions are signed; as his Holiness trusts you will be able to procure this by the excuse touching the breve. Consequently the scandal would now be so much the greater if these ambassadors come to suspect that his Holiness had given them mere words in respect to his willingness to sign the commissions, in order to gain time for you to proceed to judgement. You see how many perils this involves, both to the pope and the See Apostolic, and to all Christendom; and therefore *sustineas etiam modicum*. Be assured that his Holiness will find means to relieve you of this burden before you have sustained it so long as to feel any distress. Although this matter is important, as you know, I have perhaps used more words than necessary; but they are probably too few to express to you the pope's mind, that you are not to come to judgement on any consideration, so peremptorily did he deliver it to me.

To Cardinals Wolsey and Campeggio

Licence to proceed in the cause touching the validity of the king's marriage with Katherine, according to their commission from Clement VII, dated Viterbo, 6 June 1528, 5 Clement VII. (Great seal attached. Endorsed. Signed by the king. Windsor, 30 May, 21 Henry VIII.)

The divorce

On 31 May 1529 in the parliament chamber near the convent of the Friars Preachers, John, bishop of Lincoln presented to Cardinals Wolsey and Campeggio the commission from the pope, which was read by Florian Montini of Ferrara, notary, and accepted by the cardinals in the presence of William Claiburgh, prothonotary; Richard Watkyns and William Claiton, notaries; John Yselip, abbot of St Peter's, Westminster; Cuthbert Marshall, archdeacon of Nottingham; William Warham, archdeacon of Canterbury; Richard Doke, archdeacon of Salisbury; William Frankeleyn, chancellor of Durham; Roger Edgeworth, Henry Ratclif, John Seintcler and Thomas Arundel. (Signed by Richard Watkyns)

> Commission of Wolsey and Campeggio to persons not named to cite Henry VIII and Queen Katherine to appear before them, the time and place being left blank. (Signed by Jo. Hughes)

The cardinals then appointed John, bishop of Lincoln, and John, bishop of Bath and Wells to summon the king and queen to appear on June 18, between 9 and 10 a.m., the bishops taking an oath to perform this duty.

> Summons of Wolsey and Campeggio to Henry VIII and Katherine of Aragon to appear in the parliament chamber near the Friars Preachers, London, on Friday, June 18 between 9 and 10 a.m., and appointment of the bishops of Lincoln and Bath and Wells as apparitors.

The divorce

Papal instrument attesting that the dominical year in papal breves is computed from the nativity of our Lord, and in bulls from the Incarnation. Notarial attestation dated 31 May 1529. (Rome)

Attestation of Augustine, cardinal of St Cyriac, to the effect that only two breves were found in the Apostolic chamber relating to the dispensation of Julius II. (Rome, 31 May 1529)

Clement VII to Henry VIII

Stephen Gardiner and Francis Bryan will testify his desire to oblige the king. The king cannot doubt of his affection and his gratitude for his services to the See Apostolic, but he cannot proceed as the king desires without grave reproach. Refers him to Campeggio. (Signed "J". Rome, 31 May 1529)

JUNE 1529

The hearing in London of the case for the divorce begins, even while both English and Spanish ambassadors continue to beseech the pope to decide the matter each in their own favour. Continued lack of success in the cause brings members of Anne Boleyn's family to question Wolsey's commitment to the king. Wolsey finds himself disliked by both Katherine, for his pursuit of the divorce, and Anne, for failing to achieve it.

Bulls required
Tres instructions pro bullis obtinendis statum religionis concernentibus:

1   Instructions for obtaining a commission to erect abba-
    cies into bishoprics. A commission to be directed to
    the legates. Let it be requested on the king's behalf. Let
    a faculty be granted, in monasteries of every order, for
    the erecting of abbacies into bishoprics, dividing the
    possessions, portioning out dioceses, constituting
    archdeaconries, and uniting with them parish
    churches, and for consecrating the abbots as bishops,
    and dispensing with them for adopting the hat
    (*biretus*), rochet and other episcopal vestments.

2   Instructions for obtaining a faculty to suppress monas-
    teries of any order to the yearly value of 6,000 ducats.
    A commission to be directed to the cardinal of York.
    Let it be requested on the king's behalf. The substance
    of the request is that the pope will allow monasteries
    to the annual value of 6,000 ducats to be dissolved,
    and their possessions applied to the colleges of
    Windsor, founded by King Edward, and of St Mary
    and St Nicholas, Cambridge, commonly called King's
    College, founded by Henry VI.

3   Instructions for uniting monasteries, and for dealing
    with the monks. Let a commission be directed to
    Wolsey and Campeggio. Let it be requested on the
    king's behalf. Let the cause be the conservation of
    religion, which cannot be observed except in com-
    munities of a sufficient number; individuals scattered
    in small monasteries bringing nothing but discredit
    upon religion. Let the cardinals have a commission to
    unite, at their discretion, those monasteries which
    cannot support 12 religious out of their fruits, and
    make one perfect out of several imperfect; prescribe
    what is to be given to the poor; and shut up the nuns
    within walls according to the canons. (In the hand of
    the prothonotary Casale; endorsed by Vannes)

Monasteries and cathedrals

Bull of Clement VII for suppressing certain monasteries and erecting cathedral churches; with a *non obstantibus* clause omitted in the former bull, and for enabling the abbots to become bishops. (Sealed. Rome, 4 June 1529)

Duke of Suffolk to Henry VIII

Taking an opportunity to make known to the French king the secret charge that you gave me on his promise not to disclose it, I told him that you had been advertised by Bryan "that he should say unto the said Bryan, 'How do the king my brother's affairs concerning the divorce?' And the said Bryan should say, 'I trust well'. Upon the which he should say, 'Well, there be some which the king my brother doth trust in that matter that would it should never take effect; but I shall send Piers De Vartie (Douarty) to the king my brother, who shall disclose unto him what I know therein.'" He admits these words; says they were spoken upon communication with Campeggio, who told Francis he was going to England and afterwards to Spain by commission of the pope. On which Francis asked him how he could go into Spain, and yet do what the king of England wished for the divorce; and he replied that he did not think that the divorce would take effect, but should be dissembled well enough. Thinking that the king was deceived, he told the bishop of Bath what the cardinal had said, desiring him to advertise you of it. I then proceeded to inquire of him, promising that what he said should never be revealed, "What say you of the cardinal of England in this matter?" And he replied, "When he was with me, as far as I could perceive, he desired that the divorce might take place, for he loved not the queen; but I advise my good brother not to put too much trust in any man, whereby he may be deceived, and the best remedy is to look to his own matters himself." He said further that the cardinal of England had great intelligence with the pope and with Campeggio, and, as they are not inclined to the divorce, it is the more needful for the king to have regard to his own affairs.

No man can speak better of your grace than he does. This is all I can get from him, but I will try him again. (Orleans, 4 June 1529)

Campeggio to Salviati

After the departure of Francesco Campano on 26th May, I received your letters of the 1st, 6th and 8th of May. Owing to the protests and citations made by the Imperial ambassadors to the ambassadors of this king, the latter dispatched the cavalier Casale hither in great haste, and I believe the cavalier arrived in ten days. We had much discussion respecting the citation, as the king and Wolsey are unacquainted with the customs and forms of the papal court. At length they were made to understand the case, and became satisfied both with the citation and with the non-concession of their demands touching the brief. Nevertheless, on the receipt of your said letters, being at Richmond with the cardinal, I again explained the matter to his lordship; and by his advice I sent my secretary to Windsor to do the like with the king, and to communicate the news which you and your reverend son (in France) write to me.

My secretary reports to me that the king was not much appeased with regard to the citation made at Rome to his ambassadors, and said he was informed that it is not customary to cite the ambassadors of princes. To this it was replied that he was wrongly informed, and that the pope could not prohibit it, as the serjeants did this office, without the pope's licence or knowledge, as public officials. At my next interview with the king I will not fail to set the matter right. A copy was given them of the petition produced for signature, and of the protest; and they were made to understand that, as the Imperialists, before the coming of Francesco, had frequently urged the citation of the cause, and were still doing the same with protestations, it was sufficient that the pope, up to the present time, had not made this citation, as you prudently write. Yet the cardinal frequently inquires what I think about this citation, and I am persuaded that the pope will not make it on any account. I reply that I find the reasons alleged are very telling, and that the importunity made is infinite, so that I do not know what may be the result. Thus I leave them between hope and fear. The cardinal says he cannot believe that the pope is sending back Dr Stephen Gardiner.

They have firmly resolved that the cause shall be proceeded with. On the last day of May we performed the first act—which was to cause the bull of the commission to be presented to us, to accept the charge laid upon us by the pope, to appoint notaries and messengers to cite the parties—and the citation was peremptorily decreed for the 18th inst., Friday. The king and queen have been cited by the bishops of Lincoln and Bath, the messengers appointed and sworn for this purpose. It appears that their learned men are of opinion that we are bound by our office to proceed to execute the first portion of the bull, and you may be sure they will use all diligence to secure the speedy conclusion of the trial. I understand, though I do not know for certain, that they are consulting the theologians of the University of Paris about the case.

It is rumoured that my Lady Margaret and the French king's mother will meet at Cambray to negotiate peace about the middle of this month. The cardinal denies the truth of this, and says they will first of all arrange the particulars, and that he himself is to go there, but he will not go until this cause is expedited. The French secretary who came hither has returned.

A Polish gentleman, returning from Constantinople to the French king's service, reports that the Turk intends to invade Hungary and Germany, having an understanding with many German princes, and that the Archduke Ferdinand was in great straits and had intended to repair to the emperor in disguise, but was dissuaded from so doing.

Here we are still wearing our winter clothing, and use fires as if it were January. Never did I witness more inconstant weather. The plague commences to rage vigorously, and there is some fear of the sweating sickness. I am no longer compelled to remain in bed groaning, and therefore I consider myself in good health. (London, 4 June 1529)

Campeggio to Salviati

In my last of the 4th I announced that we had decreed a citation to the king and queen for the 18th inst. Yesterday the king returned to Greenwich—I suppose, in order to be present at the day fixed. The queen in passing crossed the water and came to visit me, even to my bedside, owing to my gout, which is accompanied by a slight feverishness— she being very anxious and perplexed about her affairs. The cause of her coming was to tell me that her advocates, who ought to have come from Flanders, had not come, because, it seemed, the emperor had given them to understand that he did not wish them to do so, as the place is not safe. Consequently, the queen found herself without anyone to plead for her; for although she had certain other English counsellers assigned her by the king, it was easy to believe that they would in everything have greater regard to the king's pleasure than to her necessity. She therefore requested my aid and counsel. In reply, I exhorted her to keep a good heart, to rely upon the king's justice, and upon the conscience and learning of those prelates who have been assigned to her for counsellors, and to rest sure that nothing inconsistent with justice and reason would be done by us. She then inquired, what was the state of the case, and how any proceedings could be taken during the trial of the cause at Rome before the pope; asking what I knew about this matter, and whether the cause had been revoked. I replied that I had learned by letters of the 15th ult. that, although great importunity had been made, the commission had not been signed, for these reasons: that the cause had not been brought into court, and that the pope, having deputed two legates for this process, would not revoke it without great forethought and consideration. I exhorted the queen to pray God to enlighten her, in order that she might take some good course in this great difficulty, considering well her state, the times and the tendency of things, and committing to God all of the greater part of her troubles. Although she is very religious and extremely patient, she does not accede in the least to these hints of taking vows. She regards this fact as the great solace of her mind and as the firm foundation of her righteousness, that from the embraces of her first husband she entered this marriage as a virgin and an immaculate woman. This she very solemnly swears. She formerly made the same declaration, and still declares and affirms it even to the king himself; and it appears that this thing raises some scruples in the king's mind. On the queen's departure from me she went to her lodging here in London and there met her counsellors. Nothing else has occurred since up to the present hour.

I communicated your last letters to the cardinal by my secretary, as also to the king, who was at Hampton Court. They did not fail to refer to what their ambassadors had mischievously written in the first instance, when they were cited, and since. I have made them all comprehend that the pope could by no means prevent the Imperialists from doing what they did; so that some of our people here assert that not even the king himself could prevent a similar act of justice being done in this kingdom. They are, however, of opinion that the pope will not sign the commission or revoke the cause; and therefore they are making the utmost importunity for it to be proceeded with and terminated.

What counsel the queen will take under these circumstances is unknown. Some think she will object to the place, some to the judges; some think to both. Others think she will not appear; others, again, that she will allege some other hindrance or impediment. Within three days we shall know for certain. I will not fail with all my ingenuity to pursue whatever course will tend to "the honour of the justice of this Holy See and of his Holiness", although I may be greatly impeded in so doing both in body and soul. In addition to my other troubles, I receive no remittances from Rome. Pray make prompt provision in order that I may not fall into dishonour by getting into debt or begging in an undesirable quarter.

The treasurer, who went to the French king with the duke of Suffolk, returned here on the 9th on account of the negotiations for this peace. I understand the French insist on an immediate determination being taken, but here there is not so much ardour as there might be. It seems to me the negotiation is being procrastinated, in order to witness the result of this cause, or at least until it is put in good trim. Cardinal Wolsey is using all his efforts to secure its conclusion, with the pope's authority. He tells me that the French king and his own king desire him to repair to Cambray for the present negotiation, and that on the completion of this business we shall go in company, and not depart without great honour and satisfaction to the pope. (London, 16 June 1529)

PS: When conversing with the cardinal about the peace, and the coming of the pope to the place of congress, he told me that the pope would not repair thither, as the French have refused his conditions, which were that Marseilles or Rouen should be placed in his hands for his security. I replied that it seemed very unlikely the pope should demand such a thing because he had no suspicion either of the French king or the emperor.

Proceedings of the legates

On 18th June the bishops of Lincoln and Bath and Wells appeared before the cardinals, produced their citation of the king and queen and declared that they had executed it, having endorsed it to that effect.

For the king, appeared Richard Sampson, dean of the Chapel Royal, with letters of proxy for himself and Dr John Bell.

The queen was herself present, and protested against the jurisdiction of the cardinals. She desired her protestation to be registered and returned to her, which the legates granted, and desired Montini, Claiburgh and Watkyns to act as notaries. They then appointed John Hewes, LLB, promotor or coadjutor; cited the queen to reappear on Monday, June 21st, to hear their decision about her protestation; and allowed Sampson to have copies of the proceedings.

Present: the bishop of Bath and Wells, the abbot of Westminster, John Tayler, master of the Rolls, and others. (Signed by Montini, Claiburgh, and Watkyns)

The divorce

1   The judges to take their seats at the appointed time and place.
2   They must receive the original letters of citation, and an attestation of their execution.
3   If the king and queen have not appeared, they must be publicly summoned.

4   The proctors of the king and queen must exhibit their proxies.
5   The judges must appoint a promotor and scribes.
6   The judge must deliver articles to each party.
7   The judge must appoint a time for them to answer.
8   They must require the notaries and witnesses to draw up an instrument of the premises.

If one party does not appear, the judges must perform the first three articles, and then pronounce the party not appearing contumacious and issue another summons for a third day that the party may receive the articles.

If the queen appears in person or by proxy, merely to protest, the judges shall assign a day to decide upon her protestation.

1   Campeggio refuses, in his own name and Wolsey's, the appeal of Katherine of Aragon to the pope, and summons her to appear on Friday next between 9 and 10 a.m.
2   Appeal of Queen Katherine to the pope, the legates having refused to accept the previous appeal by her. (Signed at top and bottom of every page)
3   Notes concerning the right of appeal from the jurisdiction of judges, and the ground on which the appeal should be granted or refused; and also concerning the appointment of scribes and selection of witnesses. (In the hand of Vannes)
4   Additional articles put in hand by the advocates of Henry VIII relative to the protest made against his marriage with Katherine in the presence of Richard Fox, late bishop of Winchester.
5   Form of summons to be used, if the queen appears personally or by proxy to protest and refuse, to summon both parties to appear to hear the decision concerning the admission or rejection of her protest.

Campeggio to Salviati

The king and cardinal are much pleased with what you write—that the protestations and commissions of the Imperialists remain in the same state, and that they had not been signed, and that Stephen Gardiner and Bryan would declare in what terms they left the matter. The king has great hope of hearing some good news for himself. The Lutheran affairs are appeased, and no one talks about them. I have returned thanks to the king and cardinal. The king replied, "Let us expedite this my business, in order that I may apply my mind to these Lutheran affairs, and then I will do all things." I believe his majesty will most certainly write, as I announced in my letter of the 4th of April.

My Lady Margaret and the regent are to meet at Cambray. Henry would wish the cardinal of York to go to the congress; but he will not go unless this cause be first terminated; which result they are endeavouring to secure with all their might. As they believe the queen will assuredly send to Rome, they intend to dispatch someone thither to supplicate the pope not to grant the citation of this cause. Among other things, the king alleges that the pope is in the hands of the Imperialists, and that it will not be safe for him to go to law at Rome.

These people are much gratified with the advices from Rome respecting the Turk, although they receive news letters from Venice. I have received great consolation from the news you give me of the pope's health, for bad news had been reported from Venice. (London, 21 June 1529)

Wolsey to Vannes and Gregory Casale

Although they are sufficiently instructed by the king's letters concerning the advocation of the cause, writes also to show them that if the king's matter is advoked at the queen's or emperor's instance, great dishonour will accrue to the king and the judges, and, if the emperor goes to Italy, the matter would never be brought to an end. They must, therefore, do all they can to prevent, and never consent to, the advocation of the cause; nor must they grant anything that may suspend or hinder the action of the legates. They must now show the king that they are of some reputation in Rome, and can do him some service.

Does not think the pope will venture to displease the king by the advocation,* and he has no cause to do so. They may assure him that if he does grant it, he will lose the devotion of the king and of England to the See Apostolic, and utterly destroy Wolsey for ever. (Westminster, 22 June 1529)

Henry VIII to Bennet, Sir Gregory Casale and Vannes
By our letters to you, and by our conference with Bennet, you were informed how it was intended that our cause should be diligently prosecuted before the legates here. They with all due ceremony directed citations for us and our queen to appear before them on the 18th, which were duly observed. But the queen, trusting more to the Imperialists than the justice of her cause, put in her protest and appealed to the pope, alleging the advocation of the cause. The judges allowed her till the 21st, when we both appeared and her protestation was refused; but she persisted in her appeal, and, when they proposed to proceed, left the court. Being thrice summoned to appear without effect, she was pronounced *contumax*, and cited to appear on Friday next. As she will make all efforts to impeach the cause, we have thought good to advertise you of the same, that you may prevent the pope from granting anything to

---

* By withdrawing the power from Wolsey and Campeggio to decide the outcome of the case.

stay process; and if the Imperialists should attempt it, you shall signify to him the dishonour he will do to his legates, his own commission, and his promises, and any other motive you can devise. We doubt not the pope will act like a loving father, and not do anything displeasant to us, knowing how inconvenient it would be for this cause to be decided at Rome, which is now in the emperor's power. You should also insist upon our prerogative, as touched upon in our letters sent by Alexander. (Bridewell, 23 June 1529)

Wolsey to Sir Gregory Casale

After I had tied up this bundle of letters and sent them to Tuke to forward, Gardiner and Bryan arrived, from whom I learned the state of the king's matters.

I find that the pope is unwilling to make any concession and will perform nothing of those things which I had promised the king, relying on the pope's kindness. At this I am greatly troubled. Although the king has great reason for abandoning the pope, and leaving him to be excluded from the forthcoming League, I will use my efforts that he shall be honourably treated; and I believe that such is his majesty's generosity that he will not fail to comply with my intercession, provided that his Holiness does nothing to the king's injury, especially in the advocation of the cause, which, among other evil effects, will cause my ruin. The pope ought not to yield to the importunity of the king's adversaries. As he will make no concession, you ought to urge him not to advocate the cause, lest thereby he loses the king and destroys my authority, reputation and life itself. I think the king will listen more readily to my intercession, if his Holiness will send good and efficacious letters *in istam sententiam*. (London, 24 June 1529)

Campeggio to Salviati

On the evening of the 22nd, Dr Stephen Gardiner and Sir Francis Bryan arrived. Owing to this the courier has tarried till now.

The cardinal of York has showed me a letter in the pope's own hand to himself and the king, containing credentials for me "respecting the premises and other public business". As I have received no letters from you, either by Dr Stephen or by Thaddeus, who arrived with them, I have not known what answer to make up to the present time, except that I have no letters, though probably they are on the way, under direction to the legate Salviati; and that as to "the premises", which referred, as it seemed to me, only to these affairs of the king, I had nothing further to say to them than to confirm what I had so frequently told them, namely, that if the pope had not done what they could have wished in reference to the brief and their other demands, this could not have occurred had the pope been able to act with justice and honour. With regard to public affairs, I reminded them that they should continue their protection and defence of the Holy See, as they had done in the past, according to the hope and faith which the pope reposed in his majesty, especially in respect to this treaty of peace.

I understand that the French king desires the presence of the cardinal of York at this negotiation at Cambray, as also does this king, but not before the termination of this cause, for which they importune beyond measure. (London, 24 June 1529)

Campeggio to Salviati

They are proceeding with inconceivable anxiety in the king's cause and expect to come to the end of it within 20 days. The queen, since she presented her appeals, has appeared no more; consequently they have a wide field for action, and entirely clear, so that they may do whatever they like and conduct the trial with all those arts which can influence the result in their favour.

Secretary of Cardinal Campeggio to Salviati

Affairs here are being despatched so hurriedly that my cardinal will be able to depart at the same time as I had intended to depart myself. Yesterday, when the cardinals sat again in judgement, the bishop of Rochester, Fisher, a man who is held here in great esteem on account of his learning and pious life, delivered an oration before the people to the cardinals, the tenor of which was, that, having by virtue of the king's commission studied this cause between the king and the queen, he had become positive that their marriage was holy and good and could be dissolved only by God; that he was prepared to die for this truth; and that if he died for such a cause, he would not believe his death to be less unjust than the execution of St John the Baptist. He presented to the cardinals a book composed by himself upon this case, for them to see. This event has given rise to much discussion; and as this man is a man of good fame, the king can no longer persist in dissolving the marriage; for this man being adverse to it, the kingdom will not permit the queen to suffer wrong. (29 June 1529)

The king's payments

Wages paid to falconers, hunters and others, by the king's commandment:

31st December to 23rd January: To Hugh Harrys, falconer, board wages from midsummer to Christmas, a groat a day; for the meat of 8 hawks, 1*d.* each, a day. To Humfrey of the privy hounds, meat for one month, 9*s.* To Christopher, falconer, for hawk's meat, 10*s.* To Bryan Talbot, part payment of his wages, 15*s.* Total January: 10*l.* 16*s.* 6*d.*

February: Board wages of Nicholas Clampe, a groat a day; his boy, at 16*d*. a week. Quarter's wages of Jo.Yardeley, hunter, 30*s*. 5*d*.; and of Parsons, "the henne takes", 45*s*. 7*d*. Total: 10*l*. 19*s*. 8*d*.

March: Quarter's wages of the gardener at Windsor, 20*s*.; William Rutter, in the forest of Windsor, 2*d*. a day; Edmond Lynde, a groat a day; 10 watermen, 10*s*. each; to Elys falconer, for the board of Henry Ellis, 16*d*. a week; board wages of John Evans, falconer, 4*d*. a day; and meat for 6 hawks, a penny each a day; John Awod, 12*d*. a day; John Notte, groom of the crossbows, a groat a day; Jasper, the gardener at Beaulie, 50*s*.; new coats for Philip and Nicholas Clampe, John Evans, Richard Brandon, Haukyn, Walter, Hugh Harrys, Thos. of London, Christopher Hawte and Old Hugh, 11*l*. 7*s*. 6*d*.; the livery coat of the purveyor of hens, 20*s*.; to Crane, the master of the children, for the wages of Robt. Pury, at 3*d*. a day; his board wages, 20*d*. a week; the gardener at Wansted, 4*l*. a year; John Rede, keeper of the great garden at Beaulie, 8*d*. a day; Robt. Elton, one of the watermen, in prest on his wages, 20*s*.; to Nic. Clampe, for keeping a lanneret called Cutte, 1*d*. a day; and other payments. Total: 64*l*. 6*s*. 4*d*.

To Humfrey Raynezford, for chippings for the king's private hounds for two months, ending 30 June, 18*s*. 8*d*., and other payments to the above-mentioned persons. Total: 21*l*. 1*s*. 1*d*.

Charles V

Is grieved that they have no hopes of obtaining their desires. Asks that letters of thanks may be sent to the Cardinal Triulcio. Wolsey's bulls are being written, and the tax will have to be paid. The illness of the Cardinal SS Quatuor had delayed the expediting of the king's bulls. His services deserve a greater recompense than a letter of thanks. Is dealing with the agents of the bishop of Palencia about Wolsey's pension. Has for some time hesitated about saying what follows. (Rome, 30 June 1529)

> [In cipher] Wolsey at one time said that unless the pope complied with the king's request, he would find some means to make his Holiness repent, and certain other expressions were used about privation. It would be good to frighten him thus, if he could be moved by threats, but Vannes sees clearly that he only fears and hopes from the emperor. Wolsey can see whether it would be better to irritate or restrain him.

EARLY JULY 1529

The hearing listens to evidence concerning the earlier marriage of Katherine and Arthur in an attempt to form judgement about its validity. Diplomacy between London and Rome reaches a frantic state, and there is concern, as always, about whether documents are disappearing on the journey.

Du Bellay to Montmorency

Begs to have his *congé*, as he wrote on the 30th ult.; otherwise, will be obliged to take it. His credit here is used up, and for his bishopric during the war he will be paid *en gambades*. The tun of three muidz of wine costs 52 cr., and he required eight tuns a month for the number who come to drink it. A good capon costs often a crown, and butcher meat (*les grosses chairs*) is twice as dear as at Paris. You may send at my expense, and see if this is not true. If they think he is extravagant, refers to Morette, who is not the worst economist in the world, and who has seen him *jusques au foye*; but this year in England is out of all reason. (London, 3 July 1529)

Has learned nothing since he wrote last. Wolsey is hidden at Hampton Court, because he knew nowhere else to go. He has fortified his gallery and his garden. Only four or five are allowed to see him.

Clement VII to Wolsey
The same to Henry VIII

Has long foreseen the difficulties of gratifying the king and Wolsey, and cannot do so without incurring manifest danger and causing a scandal to Christendom. Has written more fully to Campeggio on the subject, and Wolsey will know what he said to Bennet, who has lately come. (Rome, 8 July 1529)

Bennet to Wolsey

The pope sent for us on the 6th, though we had made great suit for an audience before, on hearing of his recovery, after long communication among ourselves, of which we have written to you in our common letter. I thought it proper to deliver to the pope the king's and your grace's letter. When he had read the letter, he said he understood that I had something of moment to impart to him. I told him your faith and observance to him were well known, and that if he complied with the wish of the Caesarians to advoke the cause, you perceived it would destroy yourself and the Church of England; that you intended to follow this cause justly, and would rather be torn joint from joint than act against your conscience. The queen could desire no more than justice, and would have it at your and Campeggio's hands as well as at Rome, and I begged him to consider the danger of making the king his enemy.

The pope answered with tears that he saw the destruction of Christendom, and lamented that he had no means of finding a remedy; that he could not satisfy the king's wish without offending his conscience and dishonouring the See Apostolic; that the Caesarians had shown a mandate from the queen, demanding the advocation of her cause, and he could not deny it.

[In cipher] Seeing we could obtain nothing from the pope, we consulted with ourselves how it might be delayed until you had concluded the cause in England. We can do no more.

If you saw the impetuosity of the Imperialists you would marvel. (Rome, 9 July 1529)

Bennet, Casale and Vannes to Wolsey

Wrote last on the 29th June. Were obliged to send the letters by Genoa, as the retreat of the Venetians left Lombardy unsafe. The following day James Salviati received letters from Campeggio, dated 4th June, but could not find out their contents, as Salviati said the cardinal complained of his showing his letter. The bishop of Feltre showed them letters from Campeggio, saying that on 1st June the commission was exhibited, and the king and queen were cited for 18th June, for which the bishops of Lincoln and Bath were appointed nuncios. The cause was being urgently hurried to a conclusion.

See clearly that the pope will do nothing to offend the emperor and is hoping to find an opportunity for settling the matter with the emperor's assent. Nothing troubles him so much as to hear that his commission is being vigorously acted on. Thought that the best course was to assure his Holiness that nothing was being done, or at least that the sentence would not be given. Told him that the citation was in consequence of the news of his ill health, lest, if anything happened to him, the jurisdiction of the legates would cease; and they were certain that the legate would not proceed to a sentence, nor would the king allow it unless he were first sure of its ratification, and of other things, which the pope must previously promise. Showed him the scandal and ruin which the advocation would cause, and think that he and Salviati will make the Imperialists acquiesce in these reasons.

Were summoned to the pope's presence on the 6th. He told them that the ambassadors of the emperor and Ferdinand had informed him that they had received letters from Lady Margaret, dated 9th June, commending the queen in the emperor's name; and they had also received a commission from the queen to act for her, in which were inserted copies of the bull of dispensation and the new brief, with the addition of a clause declaring that the marriage with Prince Arthur had not been consummated, signed by the queen. They said that the queen had written to Lady Margaret, telling her that she was unwilling to defend her cause, and she knew that great scandal and her own ruin must result, but she would rather suffer death than such an injury to her soul and her honour. She therefore desired the ambassadors to assist her as far as justice would allow. They therefore urged the pope to grant the advocation, and protested that if he refused they would seek for other remedies. They complained also of the pope's allowing the cause to be proceeded with in England, although he had promised the contrary. The pope was in great anxiety, and weeping prayed for death.

Answered that they knew nothing of the process and believed that nothing was being done, and that no sentence would be given, unless the king had every security for the result. The legates probably commenced the process on hearing of the pope's illness, to preserve their jurisdiction in case of his death. (Rome, 9 July 1529)

[In cipher] Said that the Imperialists trusted more in their clamours for justice than in justice itself, for they cannot justly complain, as the king has always shown the greatest respect for justice; the legates have done nothing unfair, and were appointed after much deliberation by the consistory, and it would be most unjust to impede them. As the king keeps justice and the fear of God before his eyes, he would be more indignant at an advocation than if the pope proclaimed war against him; the object would not seem to be justice, but the disgrace of the king, who is now left as the sole protector of the Holy See and religion. Defection of the English and French churches would undoubtedly ensue, and the Imperialists would think nothing to be more conducive to their tyranny. Said also that the pope's part was to preserve and protect what he had once granted. The pope replied that he would willingly do so, but for the present demand of the queen.

Said they did not think that the demand of an unjust and timid woman was to be attended to, as the bull of commission prevented it; and his Holiness should consider to what end he had granted the commission, whether for the cause of justice, or to inflict an injury on the king; and he must also weigh the evils that would ensue from produce. He replied with lamentations that none foresaw everything better than he; but he was so placed between the hammer and the anvil, that though he wished to please the king, the whole storm would fall on him, and, worse, on the Church of Christ. He foresaw the general ruin of

Christendom, and especially of this peace, from which he hoped so much. He had no power to apply a remedy; he had hitherto restrained the Imperial ambassadors by telling them that they had no commission from the queen, but now they exhibit a most ample commission, and say that the cause is being urgently proceeded with; and they press him for an immediate remedy, saying that the emperor's honour is more concerned than the king's, for it would be the greatest disgrace to him to allow such an insult to his family, and he therefore regards this cause more than all his kingdoms, which he says are only ornaments of fortune; but this cause touches his honour.

Answered boldly that if he granted the advocation, he would act contrary to the commission and to his promises. He said he wished to do much more than he had promised, but it was impossible that he could refuse the *signatura*, especially to the emperor, by whose power he is so surrounded that the emperor can do what he pleases with all he has.

After innumerable discussions, he concluded that he would postpone the advocation for a few days and ask to see the queen's commission, which he had not yet read, and he then might devise reasons for deferring it. Seeing that they now can only serve the king by postponing the advocation, deliberated what is best to be done to gain time for the legates to do something. Concluded to advise the pope first to write to the king, who, they thought, would answer in a just and reasonable manner; he could meanwhile show the Imperialists the evils which would ensue from this course, and he knew that the final decision of the sentence could not be pronounced.

He accordingly desired to send a courier with great haste to the king and Campeggio, which he thought would prevent matters going further than he hoped, or at least he would know for certain what was being done, and not unknowingly cause these evils. Sent Gregory Casale to his Holiness, who approved of this, but feared the Imperialists would be too importunate and vehement. He therefore sent Salviati to ask them not to press for the advocation until the pope had heard from the king. Both Salviati and the pope show great sincerity and affection to the king, and spare no labour in serving him. He could, however, obtain nothing from the ambassadors; but they vehemently cried out for justice and would hear of no delay. Sir Gregory went alone to the pope and told him that it was not his duty to consider what the Imperialists wished, but what was right; and he ought not to grant whatever they asked and refuse even the most just requests of the king. Today the Imperialist and Hungarian ambassadors most urgently begged the pope to grant the advocation next Saturday; which the pope resisted, asking them to leave the matter to him, as he would find a better way than the one they sought. They become daily more obstinate and say that it will be much better for the king to complain of the administration of justice by the pope than that the emperor should receive injustice for justice.

On the departure of the ambassadors Sir Gregory again went to his Holiness, whom he found in great consternation. After much conversation he determined to send a courier to the king, and to endeavour to entertain the Imperialists until his return; which they hope he will do.

The pope writes fully of these things to the king and Campeggio, and he requests a letter in the king's hand promising to proceed no further at present.

Received this morning letters from the king, dated London, 23rd June. In consequence of them told the pope of the citation of the king and queen, and her refusal to appear and her protestation; that a month was granted to the queen to answer, and that she placed all her hopes in the help of the Imperialists and their influence with the pope. The king therefore desired the pope to grant nothing at their request to his prejudice. Gave no further particulars, as these letters did not come by the ordinary way, and neither Salviati nor the bishop of Feltre received any. There was a packet for them with the king's letters, but the ambassadors will not deliver them unless they think it expedient.

Salviati said to Sir Gregory that there was no need to deceive him about the process, as Campeggio had written all the actions and mind of the king.

Hope, however, that even if the Imperialists cannot be prevented from producing the petition for advocation at the next *signatura*, by the goodness of the pope and the help of the cardinal of Ancona it will be postponed for a few days.

The king's cause is now at this point: The pope cannot refuse the request of the Imperialists, and all the auditors and referendarii tell him that he cannot in justice refuse the advocation. Can therefore do nothing but put it off as long as possible, and will try to do so until they hear from England. The king must therefore decide whether it would be better to suspend the process at the king's request, or to proceed to sentence before the advocation.

Vannes to Wolsey

Has received the king's and his letters dated 25th June. The packet had been opened, but the letters were untouched. Supposes, if Wolsey sent his own courier, that he must have fallen ill and sent on someone else. Omits nothing to obtain the king's desire. Knows how anxious Wolsey is about it, but they are compelled to accept not what they wish, but what is given them.

[In cipher] Have not yet delivered Campeggio's letters, that the advocation may be delayed by the pope's not knowing the particulars of which he writes. Fears much the advocation. Advises Wolsey to hasten the process, and to take care that no inhibitions or advocation is brought by way of Flanders. Will do what they can to prevent its being granted here. The cardinal of Ancona has promised that he will never assent to the pope's advoking the cause.

Sir Gregory uses the greatest diligence in the king's matters, and employs the services of his friends, who are many and of great authority. Suggests that he should be rewarded.

What he has said above about the packet being opened is not true, but he wrote it that Wolsey might show it to Campeggio if he complains of the non-delivery of his letters.

Hears from France that the king seems to protract the negotiations for peace, on account of his cause. We say that if the emperor desired peace, there is no necessity for his mixing up the king's cause with it. The Colonnese army at Perugia is disbanded for want of money; and the pope is trying to recover his own by friendly means. The arrival of the emperor is expected. The rumours about the Turk, and the defection of the Germans, daily increase. Will obtain the reformation of Wolsey's bulls as soon as he can. No servant of the king can be more devoted than Vannes, although it is his misfortune to serve him here. Asks for leave to visit his mother and family when he is recalled. (Rome, 9 July 1529)

Gregory Casale to Wolsey

Has received Wolsey's letters of 24th June and shown them to the pope. The pope is wonderfully troubled when anything is said about not advoking the cause. He did not wish at present to write to Wolsey about peace. Is ashamed to speak of the capture of the count of St Pôl and the dissolution of the French army, which was most disgraceful. On

21st June he moved his forces from Landriano, which is 12 miles from Milan, to pitch his camp five miles from Pavia. The previous evening 3,000 Spanish cavalry, with white tunics over their arms, left Milan to attack Landriano. When they arrived there it was already day, and the first body of the French had arrived at the appointed place. The Spaniards attacked the remainder and, though repulsed at first, took the town, and then pursued the other body of French, with whom were the German infantry. The Spaniards put them easily to flight and took their arms and guns. Those who had already arrived at the camp fled to Pavia. Guido Rangoni saved himself. There is no vestige of the army left. St Pôl was taken while trying to defend the guns. The French will never follow the advice of those who understand Italian affairs. Has often advised them to attack Milan while the corn was ripe; but they have not only not prevented the Spaniards from collecting the corn, but have so managed that they could not get corn from Provence without its being intercepted by the Spaniards. The Venetian forces have crossed the Adda, *sed magna ea(rum) quoque pars dissolute est, adeo ut parvo quidem numero se receperint.*

There is nothing to write about the kingdom of Naples. There is no fear now for Perugia. The Imperialists have disbanded their forces and departed. Malatesta Balionus sallied out of Perugia, and devastated two castles which had received his enemies. A secret agent of King John often visits Casale, and has told him the following news, which he received from the bishop of Zagreb, and from his servant at Buda. The Turks have crossed the Save, a tributary of the Danube, are marching on the Drave, carrying with them two bridges, and will follow the Danube to Vienna. The fleet is moving up the Danube. King John has a strong army, and the vaivodes of Moldavia and Walachia are with him. The latter's predecessor was put to death by the Turk when he deserted King John, and the present vaivode was ordered by the Turk to obey the king. With him also Albert, marquis of Brandenburg, great master of Prussia, leader of the German forces. His army consists of Hungarians, Transylvanians, Sclaves, Croats, Russians, Teutons, Moldavians, Walachians, Polacks and Tartars; and he threatens at present Styria and Corinthia, and then Austria and Vienna. All the Hungarians, Croats, Transylvanians and Sclaves who were subject to Ferdinand have joined King John. Ferdinand has only 3,500 foot remaining, the rest being routed and killed by Simon Diach and Kozka of Bohemia, King John's generals, who took all his guns. Cacianus, a Croat, Ferdinand's general, went to Vienna to collect a new army, hearing that King John was approaching with a large force, but was obliged to flee, as the people intended to put him to death for his mismanagement. He is said to have gone to King John. Ferdinand has no more forces in Hungary and has taken to Vienna the guns he had at Buda. Encloses a compendiary description of Hungary. Perhaps this sudden movement of the Turk will cause Christian princes to make peace, unless the emperor's obstinacy prevents it. If peace is put off, there will be no remedy, for the Lutherans are in arms and, against Ferdinand's will, determined in a diet to assist the Swiss Lutherans. Ferdinand's ambassador says that he must raise troops hastily on account of the approach of the Turk, as there is no time to wait for an army from Germany. He is asking for contributions of 50, 100 and 200 gold pieces from the cardinals for his master's aid. Promises to use all possible diligence in the king's cause. (Rome, 9 July 1529)

Bennet, Casale and Vannes to Wolsey

[In cipher] Wrote yesterday. In order that the pope might hear nothing of the hastening of the process, declared to him the tenor of the king's letters, and withheld

Campeggio's letters to the bishop of Feltre and Salviati. Found that it would be difficult to prevent the pope from advoking the cause at once; for though neither Campeggio nor the bishop had any news, the secretary of the duke of Ferrara showed letters from D. Florian, dated London, 25th June, stating that both the king and queen were cited and appeared; the king spoke, many ceremonies were performed; and the queen, after protesting and appealing, departed, and was therefore being proceeded against as contumacious. Supposes all this has been written to the pope, as Florian writes so openly to a person whom it does not concern. It is bad enough for the pope to know this, but much worse if it comes to the ears of the Imperialists, who, as soon as they know that the queen is being proceeded against for contumacy, will demand the advocation with threats; and they fear the pope will not wait, as he promised, for the king's answer. The secretary says that the bishop of Feltre gave him these letters of Florian's, but he denies it. Think that Campeggio would be highly pleased at the advocation, and he therefore writes about the process to frighten the pope.

Everything must be kept secret. Have asked the secretary of Ferrara to keep the above letters secret, but they do not know whether the bishop of Feltre will do so.

Documents connected with the divorce

1   Articles of the treaty between the king of Castile and Henry VII for the marriage between Arthur, prince of Wales, and Lady Katherine; articles of the treaty of marriage between Prince Henry and Katherine; articles of a treaty between Henry VIII and Francis I; another abstract of the treaty of marriage between Arthur and Katherine, 1496; letters of patent of Prince Arthur conferring a dowry on Princess Katherine, 14th November 1501; articles of the treaty of marriage

between Charles, prince of Spain, and Mary, daughter of Henry VII, 1507; a brief collection out of an account of the jointure of Queen Katherine of Spain, made for one whole year ended in the 13th year of the reign of King Henry the VIII; extract from letters patent of King Henry VIII to his consort, Queen Katherine; abstract of the second treaty of the marriage betwixt Katherine of Castile and Henry, prince of Wales, 1503; opinions respecting the divorce, *pro Rege*; two letters patent of Augustine Spinola, cardinal of St Cyriac in Thermis, dated 27th January 1529, marked *Contra*.

2   Memorandum of the production by Mr Hughes, on the 12th July 1529, of the following witnesses against the dispensation exhibited by the queen, viz., dukes of Norfolk and Suffolk, the marquis of Dorset, Viscount Rochford, the bishop of Carlisle, Sir David Owen, Sir John Hussey and Sir Richard Weston, to whom an oath was administered.

3   Hadrian de Castello to Henry VII. Written shortly after the election of Pope Julius II, of which he gives some particulars. On visiting the pope next day, he first spoke of Henry's zeal for the Holy See, and for a crusade against the Turks; then asked for a dispensation between the king's son and the daughter of the kings (*regum*) of Spain, and also for some corrections in the Bull of Indulgence.

[In cipher] The pope said the dispensation was a great matter; nor did he well know, prima facie, if it were competent for the pope to dispense in such a case, but if he could he would gladly satisfy Henry and the Catholic kings, whose ambassadors had already spoken with him.

Hadrian replied that it was quite lawful and there were excellent reasons for giving it, and said there were precedents under Alexander (VI), Innocent (VIII) and Sixtus (IV). The pope at last promised to consult with certain cardinals, of whom he named Hadrian one. Applied also for the bulls for the vacant bishoprics of Canterbury, Chichester and St Asaph's, the expedition of which the pope committed to him, as Pius III had done. News of Naples.

4   Opinion denying the pope's power of granting dispensations for marriage within the first degrees of consanguinity or affinity.

5   Notes concerning the proceedings in matrimonial cases.

6   Extracts from letters of John Hildebert, bishop of Mans, to the bishop of Seez and others, supporting the king's case.

7   Copy of a bull to the bishops of Ely, Norwich and St Asaph's, denying the lawfulness of the marriage of the prince of north Wales with the widow of his uncle, daughter of the Lord of the Isles.

8   Opinions of St Gregory, Hugo, Alexander, Peter de Palude and others, and references to passages in other authors concerning marriages of affinity.

9   "Lanfrancke, bishope of Canterburye, under kyng William the 2, brought in first Transubstantiation; and Anselm, under Henry the First, his successor, brought in unmaryed preastes; so married priests and ther impanation cannot agree, it is so pope holye, he may not toutche it; the maden preast and it must neads go together, the one cannot stand without the uther. Flores Hist, penninge this history in anno 1051, sathe it was done prope civitaten Lindiusfarne, meninge Durham, wich name is to be observed of sutche as trewlye would understand thistorye."

Katherine of Aragon

A set of depositions as to Katherine's marriage with Prince Arthur:

Deposition of George, earl of Shrewsbury, seneschal of the king's household, at the Coldherbar, on Monday, 28th June 1529. Is 59 years of age. Was present at the marriage of Henry VII at Westminster, and at the creation of Arthur as prince of Wales and Henry as duke of York. They were always considered as brothers, and he never heard it contradicted. Was present at the marriage of Prince Arthur with Katherine, now queen, at St Paul's, in November, 17 Henry VII 1521 [sic]. Believes that Arthur was then 14 or more. Saw the Queen Elizabeth and him a month after his birth, at Winchester, in 2 Henry VII. Believes that Katherine was more than 14. Thinks that Arthur must have been nearer 15 than 14. At night, with the Lord of Oxford and others, conducted Prince Arthur to the Lady Katherine's bedchamber and left him there. Supposes that the prince consummated the marriage—as he did so, being only 15½ years when he was married. They were always considered lawfully married during the life of Prince Arthur. Saw the funeral of Prince Arthur at Worcester, and the marriage of the king and queen at Greenwich. Knows that the king and queen cohabited and treated each other as husband and wife, but cannot say whether lawfully or not. Has made this deposition without being instructed or corrupted in any way, only for the sake of truth.

Deposition of Thomas, marquis of Dorset. Is 52 years of age. Was present at the baptism of Arthur and Henry—the former at Winchester and the latter at Greenwich. Was present at the marriage of Prince Arthur with Katherine, now queen, at St Paul's on a Sunday in November 1501, 17 Henry VII. Believes Arthur was about 15, for he has seen in the book in which are written the births of the king's children that he was born 20th September 1486. Was present when Prince Arthur went to bed after his marriage, where the Lady Katherine lay under the coverlet, as the manner is of queens in that behalf. Thinks that he used the princess as his wife, for he was of a good and sanguine complexion, and they were commonly reputed as man and wife during Prince Arthur's life.

Deposition of Sir Antony Willoughby. Has lived 15 years in Hampshire, for 12 years previously in Wiltshire. Was five years in the service of Prince Arthur, for five years before that in the service of the bishop of Durham, and before that time in his father's household. Was present at the marriage of Prince Arthur and Lady Katherine. By favour of his father, Lord Broke, steward of the king's household, was present when Prince Arthur went to bed on his marriage night in the palace of the bishop of London. In the morning the prince, in the presence of Maurice St John, Mr Cromer, Mr William Woddall, Mr Griffith Rice and others, said to him, "Willoughby, bring me a cup of ale, for I have been this night in the midst of Spain." And afterwards said openly, "Masters, it is good pastime to have a wife." He, therefore, supposes that the marriage was consummated; and he heard that they lay together the Shrovetide following at Ludlow. Knows that they lived together as man and wife during the remainder of the prince's life.

Examination of witnesses by John Tayler, archdeacon of Buckingham, in the presence of Florian Montini, William Claiburgh and Richard Watkyns, notaries.

Deposition of Anthony Poynes. Is 50 years of age. Was born in Kent. Has lived there, in the Isle of Wight and in Gloucestershire. Served Prince Arthur for five or six years, and subsequently Henry VII and Henry VIII. Henry VII appointed him to serve Prince Arthur as his eldest son, and he remained in his service until his death. Was present at

the marriage of Prince Arthur and Lady Katherine.
Believes the prince was above 15 years of age. Knows that
the prince and Lady Katherine lived together as man and
wife.

Deposition of Sir William Thomas of Carmarthen. Is
50 years of age or thereabout. Has lived in Carmarthen
and Shropshire for 25 years. Was groom of the privy
chamber to Prince Arthur, for three years before his
death. Henry VII and his queen always lived and were
reputed as man and wife. Was appointed and sworn servant to Prince Arthur as the king's son, and similarly to
Henry VIII after Arthur's death, and both princes received
the dignities proper to the king's sons. Was present at the
marriage of the Prince Arthur and Lady Katherine, and
they were married lawfully, as far as he knows or ever
heard. Knows that they lived together near London and
at Ludlow for five months, till the prince's death. As one
of the prince's privy chamber, often conducted him in his
nightgown to the princess's bedchamber door, received
him in the morning and conducted him to his own
room. They called each other prince and princess, man
and wife, and were always so reputed. Believes that Prince
Arthur was 15 years of age. Has been told so by Sir
William Woddall and others who were present at his baptism. Believes that the Lady Katherine was 18. Was present
at the marriage of the present king and queen in the
queen's closet at Greenwich.

Deposition of Sir Henry Guldeford. Is 40 years of
age. Can depose nothing as to the consummation of the
marriage, as he was then not 12 years old.

Deposition of Sir David Owen of Sussex, where he
has lived 40 years. Was born in Pembrokeshire. Served
Henry VII in England and abroad. Is 70 years of age. Was
present at the marriage of Henry VII and Queen
Elizabeth, at the baptism of Princes Arthur and Henry, at

their creation as prince of Wales and duke of York and at
the marriage of Prince Arthur with the Lady Katherine.

Deposition of Sir John Hussy, of Lincolnshire, 63 years
of age. Being asked as to the peace between England and
Spain, answered that there was continual peace during the
life of Prince Arthur and afterwards. Cannot say whether
it would have endured if Henry VIII had not married Lady
Katherine. King Henry VII died 20 years ago, within a
week of the feast of St George. Was comptroller of the
household, and at the court at Richmond when he died.
Was present at his burial at Westminster. Believes that
Henry VIII was 38 years of age on the eve of St Peter.

Deposition of Nicholas, bishop of Ely. Is 68 years of
age. Princes Arthur and Henry were legitimate sons of
Henry VII and his queen, Elizabeth. Was present at the
marriage of Prince Arthur, but can say nothing as to the
words used, on account of the tumult and multitude of
people there. Can say nothing as to the consummation, but
he doubts of it, because the queen has often told him, on
the testimony of her conscience, "*quod (non) fuit carnaliter a
dicto Arthuro cognita*", but they were both of sufficient age.
Believes the marriage was contracted both de facto and de
jure, by reason of the dispensation; but he cannot depose
to the time mentioned in the article. Has always believed
that it is true as to *jus divinum*, and believes that it is also
true as to *jus ecclesiasticum*. Has heard the archbishop of
Canterbury say that he had a dispute with the late bishop
of Winchester on the subject; the present king and queen
were lawfully married, as he believes. Does not consider
that the legates are competent judges, as an appeal has been
made.

Deposition of Robert, Viscount Fitzwater. Is 46 years
of age or thereabouts. Was in the service of Henry VII from
the death of Prince Arthur to the death of the king.
Princes Arthur and Henry were always considered as the

natural and lawful sons of Henry and Elizabeth. Was assigned by the king to the service of Arthur as his eldest son, and served him till his death. Was present at the marriage of Prince Arthur and Lady Katherine. Believes Arthur was then 15 years of age, as he heard from credible witnesses, and that Katherine was older. Was with the earls of Oxford and Shrewsbury and others at the bishop of London's palace, waiting on Prince Arthur going from his own chamber to that of the princess, and left him in the bed, where, he believeth surely, the princess lay. They dwelled together at Ludlow till the prince's death. As to public report, agrees with the earl of Shrewsbury. Has not been influenced by force, fear or the like.

Deposition of Thomas, Lord Darcy. Is 60 years of age or thereabouts. Henry VII and Elizabeth lived together for many years as husband and wife, to his knowledge, as he was in their service. Arthur and Henry were always considered as their lawful sons, to which he never heard the contrary. He believes that Arthur and Katherine were lawfully married, from public report. Is not influenced by force etc.

Deposition of William, Lord Mountjoy. Is 52 years of age or thereabouts. Was present at the marriage of Arthur and Katherine at St Paul's. Believes Arthur was more than 14 years of age. Knows nothing of Katherine's age, nor of the consummation, except from report. Agrees with the marquis of Dorset as to cohabitation, offspring and reputation, but cannot depose about the marriage. Never heard of any great murmur or scandal in consequence of this marriage, among either the clergy or laity. Is not influenced by fear etc.

Deposition: Katherine was then commonly considered to be older than Arthur. Has heard from trustworthy persons that they cohabited as man and wife. Was present at the bishop of London's palace at Paul's, the morrow after the wedding, waiting upon the prince at breakfast, when Maurice St John said to him, "Sir, ye look well upon the matter." To which the Prince answered, "I look well for one that hath been in the midst of Spain." From these words he believed that the marriage was consummated. Was told by Maurice St John, who was in the prince's service, that Arthur, after he had lain with the Lady Katherine, at Shrovetide after his marriage, began to decay, and was never so lusty in body and courage until his death, which St John said was because he lay with the Lady Katherine. Has not been subjected to undue influence.

Deposition of Thomas, Viscount Rochford, 15th July, at the Friars Minors. Is 52 years of age. Knows that Henry VII and Elizabeth considered the named Arthur and Henry as their lawful sons, and they were everywhere so considered. Was present at St Paul's in November, 17 Henry VII at the wedding of Arthur and Katherine; Henry VII was present in the consistory place, and a great number of Englishmen and Spaniards in the church. Believes the marriage was lawful. Arthur was above 15 years of age; which he knew from the books in which the births of the children of the kings of England are entered, and from the report of nobles present at his baptism. Heard from Spaniards that Katherine was more than 16, and she has often told him the same herself. After the marriage they dwelled together as man and wife, to his knowledge, at the king's court and at Ludleys. Believes the marriage was consummated, from their age. Heard from many who were familiar with the prince, that the day after his marriage he said he had been in the midst of Spain. The king and queen cohabited till about two years ago, when he heard that the king was advised by his confessor to abstain from intercourse with the queen, so as not to offend his conscience. Has not been subjected to undue influence. States in answer to a question that it is customary for brides, especially noble ladies, to be veiled during the blessing of the bed.

Deposition of Sir Richard Sacheverell of Leicestershire. Has lived in that county 40 years, and before that in Derbyshire, where he was born. Is 60 years of age and more. Knows that Henry VII and Elizabeth lived together as king and queen, and that Arthur and Henry were always considered as their lawful sons. He heard many people say that it was not meet that one brother should marry his brother's wife, referring to the marriage between Henry VIII and Katherine. Has not been subjected to any undue influence.

LATE JULY 1529 TO AUGUST 1529

The Treaty of Cambray sought peace between the countries of Christendom. As the congress was in progress, the pope felt able to make his decision about the divorce of Henry and Katherine.

Campeggio to Salviati

By my letters of the 21st, 24th and 29th ult., I informed you in what state this cause stood, and how it was proceeding with much celerity and more urgency. We have since progressed in the same manner with great strides till this day—always faster than a trot—so that some expect a sentence within ten days; and although we have many things to do—writings, allegations and processes to see and examine—yet the urgency and diligence is so great that nothing is sufficient to procure us a moment's breathing time. It is impossible for me not to declare my opinion, and what seems to me most convenient, but it will avail little. I will not fail in my duty and office, nor rashly or willingly give cause of offence to any person. When giving sentence, I will have only God before my eyes, and the honour of the Holy See.

The bishops of London and More departed on the 1st to attend the congress at Cambray. They had particular instructions to promote the interests of the pope and the Holy See. I believe they will use their good offices in this respect, because I did my utmost both with the king and with them. On the 2nd the capture of Mgr de St Pôl was reported here. (London, 13 July 1529)

The divorce

Fragment of a letter of Casale: The pope has revoked the king's cause. I know that nothing in the world could be more disagreeable to his majesty, especially as it was done at the request of the emperor, at this explanation with the pope. (15 July 1529)

The divorce

Deposition of Mary, wife of Henry Bourchier, earl of Essex, taken at Stanstede, on Thursday, 15th July 1529, in the presence of Robert Johnson, notary public (of Norwich diocese). Her age is 44 years and over. She says that Prince Arthur and Katherine lived as man and wife together; that the two occupied the same bed after the wedding, at London House, and were generally reputed as man and wife.

Deposition of Agnes, widow of Thomas, late duke of Norfolk, taken on Friday, 16th July 1529, in the church of

St Mary, of the Cluniac priory of Thetford, by Sampson Mychell, cannon, in the presence of John Fletcher and William Molyneux, MA, her chaplain. Her age is 52 years and over. She knew Henry VII and his Queen Elizabeth from the time she was 15, and remembers Katherine coming from Spain and the marriage of Arthur and Katherine in St Paul's. "He was then about the stature that the young earl of Derby is now at, but not fully so high as the same earl is." Also, that the said Prince Arthur and Princess Katherine, now being queen, were brought to bed the next night after the said marriage; for this deponent did see them lie in one bed the same night, in a chamber within the said palace being prepared for them, and that this deponent left them so lying together there the said night.

Bennet, Casale and Vannes to Wolsey
Write in full to the king of the state of his cause:

> [In cipher] Have left nothing undone to restrain the pope from advoking the cause; have shown him the dangers of doing so, the king's merits, the necessity of the cause, and the scandals and tumult which the advocation would produce, the ruin of the Church, and the loss of England and France. His Holiness acknowledged that all this was true. Added also the ruin that would fall on Wolsey, who had done so much for him and the Holy See. These and other innumerable reasons were of no avail; and he wished to advoke the cause without waiting to hear from the king, saying he neither could nor would wait any longer, for he had heard from Campeggio that the cause was being hastened. No one could do more than they did, but it was in vain. Therefore, on the 13th June, for this purpose alone, a *signatura* was fixed, at which the pope took the votes of the referendaries, but said that he would defer the signature until the next consistory. Found out secretly that

he signed it yesterday morning, as it would have been dishonourable to have signed it after the publication of the new treaty with the emperor, which will be published here on Sunday. Said to him that his letters to Campeggio tacitly contained the advocation, and were as effectual as this public exhibition of it. But they could not move him. He said it would not please the Imperialists, whom he could not deny. Are now urging him not to send the advocation publicly, nor to grant it to the Imperialists. This also, he says, will not please them, as they wish the advocation to come to the queen's hands, but he says he will perhaps send it by one of his household. Said that the king was being treated too ignominiously, and that the Imperialists by their boasting would do more harm than good to the queen. Will speak with the pope today, if possible. Thinks that he will yield to the Imperialists. Tells Wolsey so, that if nothing else can be done, it may be intercepted at the harbour. Wolsey sees what is to be expected from the pope if the sentence has been pronounced. His Holiness fears and trusts only the emperor. Many Imperial captains, both horse and foot, are continually passing on their way to Florence. The prince of Orange is hourly expected. Will again ask the pope that the cause may not be tried here; but they expect nothing. Are obliged to send this letter by a private courier and by an unsafe route, as no courier can go without Salviati's knowledge, and the pope does not wish the king to know anything till the advocation is sent.

Silvester Darius gives them much assistance, but everything hangs on the will of one man. (Rome, 16 July 1529)

Clement VII to Wolsey

Is very sorry to have been compelled to advoke the cause. Trusts that Wolsey will feel no regrets, considering how much the pope has done to delay it. Urges him to use his efforts to keep the king well disposed to the Holy See. Refers him to Campeggio. (Rome, 19 July 1529)

Bishop of Bayonne to Admiral Bryon

Nothing important has happened since he wrote on the 12th. Does not know how the marriage proceeds, but on Monday matters were almost as the king wishes, and the judges were deliberating about giving the sentence the Monday following. Now things are altered, and those who desired a divorce are extremely troubled, finding Campeggio not so favourable as they expected. Thinks he is inclined to remit the cognisance of the matter to the pope, *en bref ampliatif,* or else the news they have received here of the pope's illness has changed their purpose. Campeggio must have expected to have his part in the cake by doing what would be acceptable to the emperor, especially when the latter should have arrived in Italy, where it is expected he will soon be. At all events, the matter is in such a state no one can tell how it stands. We are longing very much for news from Cambray. Dare not go to court till he hear some. It is certain that if Wolsey had the power to give sentence alone, he would sooner do it than break off; but I know from sufficiently good authority that whatever he pretends the purport of the said commission to be, it is quite otherwise. "Je ne scay au vray ce qu'il en est." (London, 22 July 1529)

The divorce

Proceedings of the legatine court, containing depositions of witnesses, etc.

Depositions of the abbot of Westminster, Burbank and others of searches made in the Exchequer at Westminster, 14th July 1529. Present: Richard Warner, sub-chamberlain, and Richard Longman, doorkeeper. Also, in the orphan's chamber at Guildhall, made by Th. Tryethesley, king-at-arms, and Th. Tong, Norroy. In a great register of the latter the following words were found:

> The year of our Lord God 1502, the 2nd day of April, in the castle of Luddelow, deceased the Prince Arthur, first-begotten son of our sovereign lord, King Henry the VIIth, the 17th year of his reign; immediately after whose decease Sir Richard Pole, his chamberlain, wrote and sent letters to the king's council to Greenwich, where his grace and the queen lay, and certified them of the prince's departing; which discreetly sent for the king's ghostly father, to whom they showed this heavy and sorrowful tidings, and desired him, in his best manner, to show it to the king's highness; which, in the morning, the Tuesday next following, somewhat before the time accustomed, knocked at the king's chamber door. And when the king understood that it was his confessor, he commanded to let him in; which confessor, after due salutation, began to say, '*si bona de manu Dei suscipimus, mala autem quare non sustineamus*"—and so showed his grace that his dearest son was departed to God.

In another ancient book of calendars:

> This day was born the lord Herre, 1481 [sic], on 28 June.

And in another:

> Nativitas R.H.VIII., 28 die Junii 1491, Greenwich.
> Marriage of Prince Arthur and Katherine at St Paul's, 24 November 1501.

In the council chamber they found a printed book of the names of the bailiffs, mayors and sheriffs of the city of London, with this passage:

This year (17 Henry VII) was sent unto England the king of Spain's third daughter, named Katherine, to be married to the Prince Arthur; and she landed at Plymouth the 8th day of October, and was received into London in the most royal wise the 12th day of November, then Friday, and the Sunday following married at St Paul's Church; and an halpace made of timber from the west door to the quire door, of 12 foot broad and 4 foot of height, and in the midst of the same married; and the feast holden in the bishop's palace. And from London Bridge to Paul's in divers streets were made royal and costly pageants. And at the west door of Paul's was made a costly pageant, running wine, red, white and claret, all the day of the marriage. And at the same triumph the king made 57 knights. And the Tuesday after, all the court removed to Westminster by water, and the marriage, with all the crafts with them, in barges, with trumpets, shawms, and tabrets, in their best manner. And there the king held royal jousts, tourneys, and banquets six days after, and then removed to Richmond, etc.

Examination of Fox, bishop of Winchester, by Richard Wolman, archdeacon of Sudbury, on the 5th and 6th of April 1527, in the bishop's chamber in the castle of Wolvesaye, in the city of Winchester, in the presence of Andrew Smith, notary. Says he is 79 years old; and it is now 41 years since he knew Henry VII. Knew Prince Arthur, who was born in the priory of St Swithin's, Winchester, and baptised in the monastery—he being secretary to Henry VII, and present. Says he baptised Henry VIII in the Church of the Observants at Greenwich. Remembers the entry of Queen Katherine into London, and met her in St George's Fields and conducted her into London. Does not remember anything of the matrimonial contract between her and Arthur. Was present at the solemnisation at St Paul's. Thinks the contract was passed some time before.

Thinks the prince was of sufficient age for marriage, but cannot remember how old he was. Says they cohabited in the palace of the bishop of London, near St Paul's, for about 14 days, and after that resided in Wales, to the prince's death. After his death, negotiations took place for a marriage between Katherine and Henry, at which he was present, and had many conferences with Dr De Peohebla, Spanish ambassador. Is not certain whether Henry VII proposed the marriage. Thinks it was done by De Peohebla. How long after the death of Arthur, cannot say. Does not recollect whether any writings took place. Says that frequent deliberations took place between the king's councillors, of whom he was one, in reference to the impediment. Thinks there was a contract between the two. Does not know the express age of the prince. Is certain that a bull was obtained from the pope, which was then thought sufficient for contracting the marriage and removing the impediment. Believes that various bulls were obtained, two of which remain in England and one or two in Spain, all of the same tenor. On a copy of the bull being read to him, stating that Henry desired the marriage, and yet at the time of the bull he was a minor, believes the suggestion was a true one, so far as the peace of the two kingdoms was concerned; but whether the king desired the marriage at the time of the bull, says he does not know what the king's mind was. Says the bull was obtained by the ambassadors of the two kingdoms, and chiefly by Adrian, cardinal of St Chrysogon. Does not suppose that the consent of Henry was asked about the bull, as he was then a minor. He cannot speak of his own knowledge, but he thinks that Henry desired the marriage, and that he loved Katherine for her excellent qualities. Does not remember that Henry, when he arrived at the age of puberty, expressly consented to or dissented from the marriage between himself and Katherine. He thinks, however, that a protestation was made. Thinks this protest is still to be found with Master Ryden, clerk of the council. Does not remember that Henry VII ever interdicted the prince, after this protest, from showing signs of love to Katherine. Thinks the protest was made by command of Henry VII. Believes it was made before Ryden, the notary; and that either he, or Thomas Ruthall, or West, now bishop of Ely, drew it up, in the presence of the earl of Surrey, Dr Peohebla and Princess Katherine, at Durham Place, in the suburbs of London. Does not remember that any public instrument was made of the protest. If so, it was delivered to Henry VII. Does not think any new dispensation was gained. Says he had many conferences with Henry VII after the death of Prince Arthur, and that his intention always was that Henry should marry Katherine; but the solemnisation was put off on account of the disputes between the king and the king of Spain touching the re-demanding of the dote. Says he did not know that Henry VII ever wished to marry the mother of the present emperor, Joan, but he intended to marry Margaret, duchess of Savoy. Asked if Henry VII communicated to him any designs of other marriages for the prince, after his protest, and whether he wished him to marry the sister of the king of Spain; says he never heard of such a wish. Refers him to the laws how far the bull must be deemed sufficient.

On the bishop's declining to subscribe his deposition on account of his blindness, and none of his counsellors being allowed to be present, the said Richard Wolman said he was instructed to sign it, if necessary, in the bishop's name. Whereupon, out of deference to the king's command, he signed it.

Attestation by Augustine Spinola, cardinal and papal chamberlain, 27th January 1529, 6 Clement VII, of the breve granted by Julius II, 6th July 1504.

Copy of the breve of Julius II to Henry VII, 22nd February 1505.

Oath of Wriothesley.

Sittings on Wednesday, 21st July: Protest of Henry, prince of Wales.

Sittings on Friday, 23rd July: Prorogation by Campeggio of the court to the 1st of October.

Mai to Charles V

I have spoken with the pope, the cardinal of Ancona and the English ambassador, advising that a brief should be sent to the king, exhorting him to live with his wife, and supplying any defects that may exist in the dispensations, and commending him for his past efforts to ascertain the truth, for the safety of his conscience; but since the cause has to be removed from England, he will by this course the better remove suspicions as to his past conduct, and earn for himself the names of a just and conscientious man. I do not know if they have sent it, but, if so, I believe they have all agreed that it should be secret, *por reputacion del negocio*.

Letters from England say that they were hurrying on the affair, wither that Wolsey might go afterwards to Cambray, or for fear of the revocation. The latter cause is more likely, because they have already commissioned the bishop of London to go to Cambray. They also write that, on the 29th June, the bishop of Rochester, a very learned and holy man, had prayed publicly, and said that he was now an old man, and had studied this cause, and for discharge of his conscience he declared it a valid marriage, which only God could dissolve. Many affirmed the same opinion, and it may be that, seeing this, they will hesitate to proceed in the sentence, though I doubt it from what Campeggio writes.

I am now going to try and obtain the writings of Staphileo, a doctor of the rota, who is dead, and who was the author of that absurdity, to see on what they founded themselves, and also those which the pope has, and which they have sent him. It is now known why the English did not wish the edicts to be affixed; not merely to gain time, as I thought, but for fear of the people who wish well to the queen, as the edicts make mention of the injuries and constraint to which she is subjected.

An Imperial captain has taken a post with a number of letters which I gave to De Praet. Among them was one from the English ambassadors at Venice, saying that care ought to be taken lest the citation and inhibition should be sent. I have sent one despatch of all this by a gentleman of the queen, who has now left; another by Genoa, to Figueroa; another to the archduke of Caput, under cover from the pope, to be given to Madame. (Rome, 4 August 1529)

Treaty of Cambray

Arrangement made by Cuthbert, bishop of London, Sir Thomas More and John Hacket, with Anthoine, cardinal of Sens, and Montmorency, the grand marshal of France, whereby Francis engages, in consideration of the deliverance of his children, to accept certain obligations contracted by the emperor with Henry VIII, paying for the same at the rate of 50,000 cr. per annum. These obligations to be returned, and the arrangement to be cancelled, in the event of the children not being restored. The first instalment to be paid 1st November 1530. (Cambray, 6 August 1529)

News from Cambray, sent by Hieronymo Francho

The day before the date of this letter, the bishop of Cambray said mass. After the mass the two ladies, Archduchess Margaret and Louise of Savoy assisted by the legate Salviati, the ambassadors of King Ferdinand and of the king of England, swore to the treaty with great solemnity. The dean of Cambray announced then in a loud voice that peace was concluded between the pope, the Emperor Charles, Francis, king of France, Ferdinand, king of Bohemia, and Henry, king of England.

Afterwards a separate peace between King Henry and Madame Margaret was promulgated.

The confederates were not mentioned in this solemnity. Before leaving, the ambassadors were called to a conference, and there the article concerning Venice was shown to the Venetian ambassadors, who had not seen it before. They feel much aggravated by that article.

De Praet and Mai to Charles V

Have written how the English ambassadors were endeavouring to get the citation modified, and of our reply. Told the pope yesterday that if he wished to suspend judgement for a month, to see if the king was really inclined to justice, we were content; but that he should not suspend it so long as to make them think we were lulled to sleep, when they might seize an opportunity to revive the question, which we wanted to set at rest; that if it could be done willingly your majesty would be all the better pleased, but if not, the matter should not be left in this perplexity; and as they wished the pope to revoke the cause to his own personal decision, we besought him, without showing any diffidence, that he would not take upon himself such a disagreeable responsibility (*en aver de declarar contra gente tan delicada*); for since it was committed to the rota, and then to be referred to the consistory, his Holiness ought not to take any trouble about it.

The truth is, it would be by no means safe for the pope to take upon himself the decision; for he might die, or times might change, or, if there were nothing worse, it would encourage the English every day to ask for new decretals; for great concessions are made to them even in this day, whether it be owing merely to the pope's good faith, or to the bribery of some one of the ministers, for it is said they are very free in spending in respect of this cause. To their request that certain things in the commission should be suppressed (*que se quitasen alguns cosas de la commission*), we said if they would specify them we should be willing to concede anything that might reasonably be relaxed. Have agreed with the pope to wait and see if affairs take any new turn since the conclusion of the peace of Cambray; for this commission was of the 25th July, when the English not only had no hope of peace, but believed and wrote that it would never be concluded. (Rome, 7 August 1529)

De Praet and Mai to Charles V

This cause of England, like a young palm tree, sends forth new shoots every day. Yesterday the English ambassadors were with the pope more than two hours, and today also a good while. Have found out that they have requested that the revocation which has been made be not done in the usual form, and 'that it be committed to no one but the pope' [in cipher]. We have replied that your majesty is quite willing to defer to the king of England in everything not to the prejudice of the queen. Will speak with the cardinal of Ancona, to whom the pope has committed the matter, and see that they do not deceive us, for at the first blush it looks as if there were some trick. Here were three English ambassadors, and now two depart, leaving only the lawyer. 'It may be a sign that they mean to prosecute the cause' [in cipher]. (Rome, 18 August 1529)

Wolsey to Gardiner

Sends him letters received this day from the bishop of Bath to be shown to the king, showing that the bishops of Bath and London had broken with the queen. There is good hope that the queen will be induced to conformity. Though the bishop of Bath refers for further particulars to my lord of London, Wolsey cannot write more, as the latter, coming hither yesterday with Mr More, chancellor of the duchy of Lancaster, fell from his horse and is since unable to travel. Will write when he has seen him. Daily expects to hear the king's pleasure on the points mentioned in his other letters, especially for the publication of the peace, and making fires and other rejoicings for it.

Gardiner to Wolsey

Would have shown your letters to the king immediately if I could have had an opportunity, but had none, as it is our removing day. The matter contained in them has been reported already by the bishops of Bath and London. I have not yet learned the king's pleasure, except for the proclamation of the peace in London and Calais with the same solemnities as in France. The coming of Langes keeps the king in suspense, except that he has told me something of his mind to be written to the bishop of Worcester. (Woodstock, 24 August 1529)

SEPTEMBER 1529 TO EARLY
OCTOBER 1529

The recall by the pope of the case to Rome, and his decision not to reverse the judgements of Pope Julius, means that the hearing in London is of no value and can have no effect.

Erasmus to More

Is delighted with the rumours of peace, for which they are indebted to Henry VIII. Speaks very highly of King Ferdinand, who has invited Erasmus to Vienna. The Turk is invading Hungary. Wishes the emperor would assist his brother and sister. I am afraid he is staying too long in Italy, but I doubt not that he will show all respect to the sovereign pontiff. It does not appear to me to be expedient for Christendom, or for the pope himself, that he should be mixed up with these princely alliances. I should like to see again the dear friends whom Holbein has exhibited in his picture. (Fribourg, 5 September 1529)

Erasmus to Margaret Roper*

Cannot express the delight which he felt on receiving Holbein's picture of the More family. Recognised everyone in it, none more than herself. Methought I saw a soul shining through this most beautiful household even more beautiful. Sends her a letter from a chaplain to Mary, formerly queen of Hungary. Begs his letter may be shown to her sisters, and his compliments to her mother Louise. I have kissed her picture, as I could not kiss herself. My best wishes to your brother John More, and your husband Roper. (Fribourg, 6 September 1529)

Stephen Gardiner to Wolsey

The king desired me to write to you that, partly on your advice and partly of his own opinion, he has answered De Langes. The copy of the answer, signed by my hand, I now send, adding "totts" in the margin, that you may perceive all that is in his mind. So when the French ambassadors resort to you, you must say to them conformably as has been said here. If the ambassadors should desire to have a letter from the king to their master of like tenor to that sent by the duke of Suffolk, for which they have pressed the king and been put over, the king desires you to satisfy them, and make some excuse.

Yesternight, I read to the king your letters in answer to mine concerning the execution of the letters citatorial.

---

* Margaret Roper was the daughter of Sir Thomas More.

He gives you his most hearty thanks for your labours in that behalf, and desireth much to know the further resolution in that matter; and when your grace writeth of the deliverance of Cardinal Campeggio's letters and breves to him directed, I assure your grace there came never so such to my hands. Yesterday, letters arrived from Rome, directed to the king and others. Probably the packet was broken up, but the letters were not opened. The king opened all; and as they are much in cipher, he desired they may be deciphered and remitted here. The king desires the prior of Reading, who is now in prison for Lutheranism, to be set at liberty, unless the matter be very heinous..

The ambassadors of France have taken their leave, and are on their way to you. (Woodstock, 7 September 1529)

Stephen Gardiner to Wolsey

I have caused Bonner and Kerne to speak with the king, who likes your device for superseding the cause, if the queen can be induced thereto, and he trusts to your dexterity. If this cannot be, he is content the inhibition should be executed upon you and Campeggio, as he has told Bonner and Kerne. (Woodstock, 8 September 1529)

Stephen Gardiner to Wolsey

On the arrival of your servant, Forrest, I repaired to the king, and read him your letters. The first part of which, showing how you had induced the queen's counsel to be content with exhibiting the brief, instead of the letter citatorial, was very agreeable to him. He hopes, if the queen should afterwards retract, she shall not be able to do so, but this her act, done before you and Campeggio, may prevent her from proceeding at Rome, or gaining any citation hereafter. With regard to your request for a personal interview with the king, he was somewhat troubled, being not able to conjecture what the matter should be you could

not as well commit to writing; and he desired me, therefore, to despatch Curzon to you, desiring to have under
your own hand the *caput rei* which you mean, whether it
be foreign or domestic; and if the former, touching what
potentate; and if relative to the divorce, the briefest note of
it; or relative to the realm, so to touch it that you can
explain it further when you arrive and relieve the king
from this agitation. (Woodstock, 12 September 1529)

Sir Thomas More to Mrs Alice (Lady More)
I am informed by my son Heron of the loss of our barns,
and our neighbours' also. The loss of so much corn is a pity,
but we must not only be content, but be glad of God's visitation. Perhaps we have more cause to thank Him for our
loss than for our winning, for His wisdom sees best what
is good for us; so pray be of good cheer, and take all the
household to church, and thank God both for what He has
given and for what He has taken from us. I pray you to
make some good ensearch what my poor neighbours have
lost, and bid them take no thought therefor; for if I should
not leave myself a spoon, there shall no poor neighbour of
mine bear loss by any chance happened in my house.

Begs her and the children to be merry, and consult
with friends about providing seed corn for the coming
year. Expected, on coming here, to remain with the king;
but intend now to get leave next week and come home.
(Woodstock, 13 September 1529)

Tuke to Wolsey
Have heard that my poor wife is sore vexed with a passion
in iliis. She has been once or twice in danger of her life, but
being at London had speedier remedy than she can have in
a village. I have obtained leave to see her and return to the
king at Windsor. The instructions for Mr Boleyn and
Carew are written. The letter to Lord Dacre has been

signed and sent. I have also written to Ichingham, and I have left here letters in French ready made to the French king and my Lady, in recommendation of Cardinal Campeggio. (Grafton, St Matthew's Day, 1529)

The king's progress

The progress of King Henry VIII, made in the 21st year of his reign:

July 1st at Bridewell; 6th at Greenwich; 8th at Bridewell; 15th at Durham Place; 28th at Greenwich.

August 2nd at Waltham; 11th at Barnett; 14th at Tytynhanger; 16th at Olborne; 17th at Windsor; 21st at Reading; 23rd at Haseley; 25th at Woodstock.

September 1st, at Langley; 4th at Woodstock; 9th at Buckingham; 10th at Grafton; 24th at Buckingham; 25th at Notley; 28th at Byssham; 29th at Windsor.

Henry VIII to Clement VII

On the return to your Holiness of Cardinal Campeggio, we could have wished, not less for your sake than our own, that all things had been so expedited as to have corresponded to our expectations, not rashly conceived, but owing to your promises. As it is, we are compelled to regard with grief and wonder the incredible confusion which has arisen. If the pope can relax divine laws at his pleasure, surely he has as much power over human laws.

Complains that he has often been deceived by the pope's promises, on which there is no dependence to be placed; and that his dignity has not been consulted in the treatment he has received. If the pope, as his ambassadors write, will perform what he has promised, and keep the cause now advoked to Rome in his own hands until it can be decided by impartial judges and in an indifferent place, in a manner satisfactory to the king's scruples, he will forget what is past and repay kindness by kindness, as Campeggio will explain. (Windsor, 30 September 1529)

Wolsey's household

The *tertii denarii* arising from beef and mutton consumed in the household of Cardinal Wolsey for one year. The amount of animals killed is as follows: 430 oxen, 181 muttons in the month of October; 728 ditto within November; 621 ditto between Easter and 1st August; 363 ditto between 1st August and 30th September. Sum total of the third pence, 204*l*. 17*s*.

My lord cardinal, pro pellibus multonum.

The divorce

Petition of John Antony Muscetula, Imperial ambassador, to the pope, in the name of Katherine of Aragon and the emperor, to advoke and decide the king's cause, and impose on him perpetual silence, or at least to commit the judgement to cardinals at the court of Rome or papal auditors, as it is notorious that the queen cannot be defended or obtain justice in England; and to forbid anything to be done prejudicial to the cause, or a fresh marriage to be contracted by the king, under the penalties of ecclesiastical censure, to be assisted by the secular arm if need be.

Vannes to Wolsey

Disputes have arisen in London between the merchants of England, Italy, Flanders and Spain in consequence of the public edict about the value of gold; for many say that debts contracted before the proclamation must be paid at the rate of 22*s*. to a pound, 14*s*. 4*d*. to a mark and 7*s*. 4*d*. to a noble, whether paid in silver or gold. Merchants also now abstain from exchanges, and thus prevent the importation of gold. Knows of the importation of 100,000 cr.

and 10,000*l.* in gold, which will be exported again unless care is taken. In Flanders, directly after this proclamation, gold was publicly put at a higher price than before; a noble at 24 gr., a royal at 35 gr. and a crown at 14 gr. The searchers should, therefore, be warned to attend to their duty.

Has sent an account of the errors, and the accounts relating to merchandise, in Italian, as he cannot trust any one to translate them into English.

The merchants ask Wolsey to intimate his wish about the proclamation to the mayor of London, that he may publish it.

Asks Wolsey to remember his affairs when he sees the king.

Katherine of Aragon to Charles V

There came hither with Campeggio a doctor of law, a native of Barcelona, who has been 30 years in the rota of Rome and lost everything he had when Bourbon entered the city, so that even now he is in great poverty. Requests Charles to give him some preferment in Naples. (Windsor, 2 October 1529)

The divorce

Notarial attestation, by Tho. Argall and John Cock, of a transumpt of a papal bull, dated Rome, 29th August, declaring that all censures and penalties against the king are invalid and contrary to the pope's intentions. (5 October 1529)

Clement VII to Henry VIII

Has suspended his cause. Assures him that the dispensation was a positive and not a divine law; and if the queen, as she affirms, was not known by Prince Arthur, there is no doubt that the dispensation was perfectly sound *in foro conscientiae*. Begs him to consider the danger in which Christendom stands from the Turks, and how much it is enhanced by this dispute. (Rome, 7 October 1529)

Campeggio to Salviati

You will have been many days without letters from me, because, having written many times and received no answer, I suspect that my letters have been intercepted; though, indeed, owing to the absence of the king and the cardinal of York, I have had nothing worthy of communication. I had notice of the revocation, citation and inhibition. I therefore expected that the letters and authentic breves would arrive, and would enable some act to be performed by which the hands of us legates would be tied, as nothing else remained for me to do; and then I could take leave.

While in this expectation, I was requested by the cardinal of York to repair to a town of his, called the More, where he has a very fine palace. I went there accordingly. On the day following my arrival, which was on the 5th ult., two breves were sent from the king's court to the cardinal, both of the same date, I think the 19th of July; the one concerning the confederation made with the emperor, the other concerning the citation. Seeing that both contained credentials for me, and that no other letters appeared, I was somewhat annoyed. All diligence was used to discover them, but there was no order, and they excused themselves saying that they had not reached their hands. The breves, however, came in time, because they supplied the means of intimating the citation in such a manner as to tie the hands of us legates. There was much to be debated, both on the king's part and on the queen's. At length the form of intimation was agreed upon, and it was made to us by a proctor of the queen's, who announced that we had no powers and that neither of us could proceed any further.

This done, I sent to request an audience of the king, which was deferred a week, owing to the arrival at that time of an ambassador from the emperor. Meanwhile the duplicates arrived of your letters of 19th and 23rd July, continued to 1st August. The originals, which you announce having dispatched with the capitulation, had never reached me. I repaired therefore to the king at the appointed time. The day before, by good fortune, I received your two last letters of 12th August and 2nd September, with the breve for his majesty touching the revocation of the censures and pecuniary penalties, and the suspension of the cause till Christmas. On these subjects I held a long discussion with his majesty, and communicated to him so much of the letters as seemed to me suitable to the purpose. The king said very little about the confeder-ation, neither praising nor objecting to it. With regard to the citation of the cause, *per le cose precesse*, he exhibited much displeasure and complained of the pope and myself for giving him words only. When I explained to him the causes of the citation, he replied in these exact words (in Latin):

> Your people (*vestry*) know very well how to accommodate
> their words to the times, but you also know it was
> intimated to me from Rome that I ought to procure
> sentence, after which the matter would assume a different
> complexion.

I replied to him that as for myself no information touch-ing this matter, wither directly or indirectly, had ever reached me; that I believed it was the same with the pope, as I should certainly have heard something about it; and that if it had been written to him by others, I was not responsible for it. I have since been in doubt about the matter of great importance which Dr Stephen Gardiner, as he wrote from Rome, said he had to communicate to his majesty, but I have been unable to arrive at the truth. Whatever it may be, as his majesty is of this opinion, and is persuaded by others that the marriage is null by divine law, his mind cannot but be somewhat enraged and disappointed because the affair has not succeeded to his liking. In other things, the king's mind is good. He has told me, with apparent sincerity, that he would never fail to be a most Christian king. In this conversation I alluded to the Lutheran affairs, and to this parliament which is about to be holden, and I earnestly pressed upon him the liberty of the Church. He certainly seemed to me very well disposed to exert his power to the utmost.

After this I presented the breve. It proved very acceptable to him, and he read it through with great attention. I know that, when reading it to his councillors, he declared that he felt highly satisfied with it. Among other things he was pleased with the clause in which the pope exhorts him to treat the queen well. His majesty remarked in Latin, "see, although his Holiness is able to command, he merely exhorts." In fact the breve greatly soothed his mind; and in order to improve the occasion, I again assured him of our Lord's good mind towards his majesty, and that he might confidently promise himself all that the pope could possibly do for his benefit. It seemed to me expedient, to avoid a greater evil, to entertain him with some hope, and I think it would not be amiss if the same were done from Rome. Lastly, he gave me a kind of dismissal. On returning home I was attacked with a pain in the side, together with the gout, which have tortured me ceaselessly for ten days; in which, however, I have collected my baggage, and departed on the 5th from London. Today I reached Canterbury, through which the auditor of the chamber (Ghinucci) is passing, to whom I deliver this letter; and as he is in a hurry, and you will learn more fully from him the state of affairs here, I will write no more. With all my heart I thank the pope for his good mind towards me.

The grand ecuyer and Dr Sampson, ambassadors to the emperor, are now passing. I learn from a good source that the king has charged them to ratify the League, even though the French king refuse to do so. It is my opinion that, on the recovery of the French king's children, this peace will not endure very long. (Canterbury, 7 October 1529)

OCTOBER 1529 TO DECEMBER 1529

The fall of Cardinal Wolsey

Wolsey to Henry VIII

Though I daily cry to you for mercy, I beseech that you will not think it proceeds from any mistrust I have in your goodness, nor that I would molest you by my importunate suit. The same comes of my ardent desire, that, next unto God, I covet nothing so much in this world as your favour and forgiveness. The remembrance of my folly, with the sharp sword of your displeasure, have so penetrated my heart that I cannot but say: *Sufficit; nunc contine, piissime Rex, manum tuam, &c. Beati misericordes, quoniam ipsi misericordiam consequentur:* which, that I may obtain, I shall not cease to pray as your most prostrate poor chaplain, "T. Car^{lis} Ebor., miserimus".

Wolsey to Montmorency

Campeggio is still at Dover and I have just heard that, on pretence of want of ships, they will not let him pass without consulting about it, for fear he carries off the treasure of the cardinal of York.

Du Bellay to Montmorency

I have visited the cardinal in his troubles. He is the greatest example of fortune that one could see. He represented his case to me in the worst rhetoric I ever saw; for heart and tongue failed him completely. He wept, and prayed that Francis and Madame would have pity upon him, if they found that he had kept his promise to be a good servant to them so far as his honour would permit. But at last he left me, without being able to say anything more to me than his countenance did, which has lost half its animation. His case is such that his enemies, even though they be Englishmen, could not help pitying him, yet they do not desist from persecuting him to the last; and he sees no means of safety, unless Francis and Madame will help him. He does not desire legateship, seal of office or influence, is ready to give up everything to his shirt, and to go and live in a hermitage, if this king will not keep him in disfavour. I have consoled him as well as I could, but I have been able to do little. He has since sent to me, by one whom he trusts, to show what he would wish done for him, saying that it would not hinder Francis if he at least wrote to this king that there is a great rumour in France that he had removed Wolsey from his presence and from his good favour, so that he was in danger of being destroyed, which Francis could not readily believe, and hoped Henry would not suddenly take up a bad impression against those who have seen that he was the instrument of this perpetual amity, so renowned throughout Christendom; and that if, perchance, he had fallen into his displeasure, he hopes the king will moderate his anger, which he is sure he will be counselled to do by those about him who have the management of his grace's affairs. This was the most reasonable of all his requests; in which I hope I am not obtruding my advice if I say that such a letter ought not to be taken ill by any man here, especially when they consider, as they do, that they are compelled to take your part more than ever.

Moreover, I assure you that the greatest advantage they have ever had of him, and what has served most to put him in discredit with the king, was that at my coming he declared too openly his wish to go to Cambray. The others persuaded the king that this was only to escape from being at the expedition of the marriage; and I can tell you that without him they were terribly near bringing the king to break off the peace negotiations. So I wrote to you at the time; but I left ten times as much to say, which I must keep till I see you, and which I am sure you will find very strange. If the king and Madame think this advisable, they will have withdrawn a faithful servant from the gates of hell. But he begs above everything that this king be not informed that they have been asked to do it; for his enemies insinuate that he has always had, both in peace and war, secret intelligence with Madame, from whom during the war he received large presents, and that this was the reason why, when Suffolk was at Montdidier, he did not help him with money, which would have enabled him to take Paris. This they talk of in a whisper, that I may not be apprised of it. As to the said presents, he hopes Madame will not do him an injury if it be spoken of. In all other things he recommends himself to her grace. These lords intend, after he is dead or ruined, to impeach the state of the Church, and take all their goods; which it is hardly needful for me to write in cipher, for they proclaim it openly. I expect they will do fine miracles. I have also been told by your great prophet with the brazen face, that this king will hardly live more than . . ., to whom, as you know, so far as I see by his writings, he has allowed no further term than the monster of May.

I must not omit to say that if Francis and Madame wish to do anything for Wolsey they must make haste. The letters will never be here before he has lost the seal. But he no longer cares about that. They will help for the rest. Also they should give my successor, whom every one is expecting here in a few days, charge to speak about it. The worst of his evil is that Mademoiselle de Bullen has made her friend promise that he will never give him a hearing, for she thinks he could not help having pity upon him. (London, 17 October 1529)

Henry VIII to Campeggio

I have read your latter letters, in which you complain grievously of the disrespect shown to the pontifical dignity, and the violation of your legatine authority, because certain porters of ours have examined your baggage; and a rumour has prevailed that you and the cardinal of York had been guilty of collusion in our cause; and that you would not leave England until this calumny had been cleared up and satisfaction given for so atrocious a wrong. I cannot sufficiently wonder that your wisdom should exaggerate such minute offences, and take such dire offence, as though it were in my power to anticipate the temerity of the mob or the excessive officiousness of others in discharge of their duty. As to your legateship, no wrong has been done by me or mine, seeing that your authority only extended so far as to the termination of my cause; and when that was revoked by papal inhibition, it had expired; and neither I nor my subjects acknowledge that you have any other authority. I wonder that you are so ignorant of the laws of this kingdom that you were not afraid to make use of the title of legate when it became defunct, seeing that you are a bishop here, and so bound by the most solemn obligation to observe and respect my royal dignity, jurisdiction, prerogative, etc.

As to the business of the porters, long before your return into Italy they had received orders to allow no one to pass on any legal suspicion, even with our letters patent, without diligent examination of their baggage. As we had no intention that this should prove an annoyance to you, nor hinder your journey, or cause you any loss, we request that you will take this in good part; and we regret that greater caution and prudence was not shown by the officers in discharge of their duty. As it was done in fulfilment of their oath, we trust you will not consider them deserving of punishment. You will do us wrong if you think the worse for this fact.

As to the other part of your complaint, touching the rumour which has arisen, it would be hopeless for you to stay here in the expectation of removing it by any process. A wise man will pay no attention to ordinary rumours. You may infer from it that my subjects are not very well pleased that my cause has come to no better conclusion. I shall have reason to doubt your faith and the integrity of your friendship when your words and professions so little agree. (Endorsed by Gardiner; and by Boleyn. Windsor, 22 October 1529)

Cardinal Wolsey

Indenture between the king and Wolsey, by which the latter acknowledges that on the authority of bulls obtained by him from the court of Rome, by which he was made legate, and which he published in England contrary to the statute, he has unlawfully vexed the greater number of the prelates of this realm, and other of the king's subjects, thereby incurring the penalties of *praemunire*, by which also he has deserved to suffer perpetual imprisonment at the king's pleasure, and to forfeit all his lands, offices and goods.

He prays Henry, in part recompense of his offences, to take into his hands all his temporal possessions, all debts due to him, and all arrears of pensions and presentations to benefices, and covenants to make further assurance when required. (Signed by Wolsey. Remains of his seal attached. 22 October, 21 Henry VIII)

Du Bellay to Montmorency

Would be glad to grant to Wolsey the request which he made to me secretly by an Italian servant, the only one who has remained faithful to him. On Tuesday the great seal was taken from him, and an inventory was made of his goods, and commands were issued to everyone who had been in his service these 20 years to render an account of all that they have touched. This they have found difficult, because, not a sixth part being found of what was expected, they are well assured to have many *tours de corde*. He was also ordered to reply before the king or parliaments; and thinking, what is quite true, that the bishops had already chosen judges after their own liking for the said parliament, he preferred to put himself in the mercy of the king; of which nevertheless he hoped less than nothing, being used with such severity that, in addition to the loss of all his goods and honours, he expects to be perpetually imprisoned, and that neither the king nor parliament will ever revoke his sentence. The points of which he is accused are robberies and exactions, but these

would not be mortal offences. They say at Amiens he
agreed to admit the duke of Ferrara into the League, without the knowledge of the king; that he delivered to Francis
a bond under his hand without authority; that he made
intimation of war to the emperor, etc. The least of these
things, they say, will cost his head; and I fully believe that
if Francis and Madame do not help him in all diligence, he
is in great danger. He would like Francis and Madame to
send a gentleman hither in all diligence, by whom they
would represent what you wrote on the 16th, without
specifying further, or giving the least intimation that it was
at his request, otherwise it will be immediate death to him.
He begs Francis, for the mercy of God, thus to protect him
from the fury of his enemies, who would bring his old age
to the most shameful and miserable end. For my part,
though I have no business to meddle further, or to give my
advice, I will say little, knowing that where affection and
pity reign the judgement is apt to be biased. The duke of
Norfolk is made chief of the council. (London, 22 October
1529)

Du Bellay to Montmorency

[The beginning of the letter is in cipher; undeciphered.]
While writing, I have heard that Wolsey has just been put
out of his house, and all his goods taken into the king's
hands. Besides the robberies of which they charge him,
and the troubles occasioned by him between Christian
princes, they accuse him of so many other things that he is
quite undone. The duke of Norfolk is made chief of the
council, Suffolk acting in his absence, and, at the head of
all, Mademoiselle Anne. It is not known yet who will have
the seal. I expect the priests will never have it again; and
that in this parliament they will have terrible alarms. I
expect Dr Stephen will have a good deal to do with the
management of affairs, especially if he will abandon his

order (*jetter le froc aux horties*). But I am not so much disgusted but that, if any one offered me Paris and St Mor, I would take them, and be at the charge of being your bishop. I am, however, compelled to tell you that I am here in the greatest dishonour, which will increase when the whole parliament shall meet, especially seeing I must ride on a mule for fear of the plague, which has visited the animals; and I do not think that you wish me to renew my train and refurnish my house, which you know is impossible. (London, 22 October 1529)

PS: They are vexed at not hearing news from you more frequently, and are very anxious to hear some to the disadvantage of the emperor, either by means of the Turk or otherwise.

Wolsey's colleges

Fortnightly accounts of building expenses for Cardinal's College:

Stone is taken from Cotswold and Heddington. Payments for new lodges made for freemasons at Barrington and Shurburne; expenses at Sonning; carriage of gravel; repairing lime-kilns at Beckley; taking down lead at Wallingford; carriage of lead from Poughley; felling, hewing and squaring timber; new frame wrought for the almshouse at Kirtlington; "bartering of toles" at Burford; purchase and "bartlage" of "wainscoats"; paring tiles and plaster; painting and gilding the hall "and greffith for the femerall"; besides wages to freemasons, "herdhewers", carpenters and other labourers.

Wolsey to Henry VIII

These shall be to thank you for the comfort sent to me, languishing in extreme sorrow and heaviness, by Sir John Russell, by which I perceive you will have pity and compassion upon me. I shall endeavour as well as I can to

attemper my sorrow, praying that, as soon as it will stand
with your honour, it may be openly known to my poor
friends and servants that you have forgiven me mine
offences and delivered me from all danger of the laws.

Cardinal Wolsey

Memorandum of the surrender of the great seal by
Cardinal Wolsey, on 17th October, to the dukes of Norfolk
and Suffolk, in his gallery at his house at Westminster, at 6
o'clock p. m., in the presence of Sir Wm Fitzwilliam, John
Tayler and Stephen Gardiner. The same was delivered by
Tayler to the king at Windsor on the 20th October, by
whom it was taken out and attached to certain documents,
in the presence of Tayler and Gardiner, Hen. Norris, Thos
Heneage, Ralph Pexsall, clerk of the crown, John Croke,
John Judd and Thos Hall, of the Hanaper.

On the 25th October the seal was delivered by the
king at East Greenwich to Sir Thomas More, in the presence of Hen. Norris and Chr. Hales, attorney general, in
the king's privy chamber; and on the next day, Tuesday
26th October, More took his oath as chancellor in the
great hall at Westminster, in presence of the dukes of
Norfolk and Suffolk, Th., marquis of Dorset, Hen., marquis
of Exeter, John, earl of Oxford, Hen., earl of
Northumberland, Geo., earl of Shrewsbury, Ralph, earl of
Westmoreland, John, bishop of Lincoln, Cuthbert, bishop
of London, John, bishop of Bath and Wells, Sir Robert
Radclyf, Viscount Fitzwater, Sir Tho. Boleyn, Viscount
Rocheforde, Sir Wm Sandys, Lord Sandys and others.

Chapuys to Charles V

On the receipt of your letter on Thursday the 21st, dated
Piacenza, I sent to Windsor to ask for an audience. As the
administration has fallen principally into the hands of the
duke of Norfolk, and the communication is more agree-

able to him than that of the marriage, I hastened to visit him. The cardinal, who was dis-evangelised on the day of St Luke the evangelist (18th October), has been deprived of his offices. I was received by the duke with great distinction, and expressed to him the regard in which you had always held him for his goodwill. He seemed highly pleased, and said that he and his family had always been attached to the house of Burgundy; that no one more lamented the late disagreements than himself, but that all the evil and misunderstanding ought to be attributed to those who formerly directed the king's councils, acting by their own will and authority, with which the king himself was often dissatisfied.

In reply to his remark that he should like to serve your majesty against the Turk, I praised his virtuous feelings, and told him that was the main object of my communication; but for the better security of peace, which the king had done so much to establish, one unhappy difference between himself and the queen remained to be settled. I told him that, however strongly he might feel from family considerations, he could not but feel as a true knight, nor act otherwise than if it had been his own daughter, and as conscience directed; and that your majesty was convinced that he had not been the promoter of this step. He replied that he would sooner have lost one of his hands than that such a question should have arisen; but it was entirely a matter of law and conscience, and he had never been appealed to; that it had been submitted to ecclesiastics and doctors, who had pronounced against the validity of the marriage; that if the dispensation you held was illegal, the king would consider himself the most abused prince in Christendom; and that if you had declared yourself in it so openly, it might have sooner been brought to a satisfactory issue. I explained to him the constraint under which you acted; and that, as to the king of England not having

declared himself a party in the matter, it was clear that he
had done so from the proceedings of the English ambassadors at Rome. Finding he remained thoughtful, I
changed the subject. Shortly after, he turned to me with a
laugh and said, "How glad the emperor will be to hear of
this fall of the cardinal, and his loss of office?" I answered,
I thought you would, but not from any hatred you had to
the cardinal; and that he could have done neither good nor
ill to you, and was not of such importance as that you are
to be avenged, or trouble yourself about his disgrace; but
what you rejoiced at was that the king of England would
now learn who had been his evil counsellors, and leave the
management of affairs to men who from birth and circumstances were more competent. I told him that I was
the first who had broken through the chain of paying
court to the cardinal, and addressed myself to him.

He thanked me for my good intentions and said that
the government was managed not by an individual but by
the council, where he usually assisted, and would promote
your majesty's interests.

In order to please the duke I asked him what I should
do, although I had already sent one of my secretaries to the
king. He told me that the king had ordered that application should be made direct to himself, before any other
person was acquainted with the communication. He followed me to the hall, using very courteous language.

On the 22nd my secretary returned from Windsor,
stating that the king would be at Greenwich on Saturday
and I was to go the day after. On my reaching Greenwich
I found a civil gentleman, named Bollen, sent by the king
to conduct me to the palace. There I found the bishop of
London, who led me to the king's antechamber, where the
court was assembled, and was received by two dukes and
the archbishop of Canterbury. I conversed with these lords,
waiting for the king to go to mass; and we talked of the

conference at Bologna. The king, on going to mass, came directly to me and taking me by the sleeve said with the utmost graciousness, "You have news from my brother the emperor?" On answering Yes, he asked the date, and then said your majesty was very careful to give him information. I assured him that you were anxious to make him partaker of all affairs and thus show your brotherly affection. I then presented your letters, and, as to the particulars of my credentials, he said that the ambassadors in your court were authorised to treat about them. Speaking of your going into Italy I bespoke his good offices.

On his return from mass, he came up to me again and resumed the subject. When we talked of the necessity of resisting the Turk, and of the pope's arrival at Bologna on the 5th, I said I thought it advisable that he should commission his ambassadors with the pope to treat; and I combated his remark that he could do but little against the Turk, seeing he was wealthy and as absolute in his dominions as the pope. He urged that this affair was chiefly yours, and if you wished to accomplish it you must make peace with the princes of Italy. I assured him you had never ceased from efforts in this direction. The conversation then turned on the Duke Francesco Sforza; and I urged, in opposition to his remark, that your proceedings were as favourable to the duke as could be. He objected to the cession of Pavia and Alexandria, alleging the cruelties which had taken place at Sienna. I told him Pavia was out of dispute, as it was already given up. "Between ourselves", said he, "I think it is a great shame that whilst the Turk is in Austria, the patrimony of the emperor, he should not rescue it, but make war upon Christians." On my urging the danger that might be expected from Sforza and the Venetians if your troops were withdrawn, he urged that neither could do anything. Shortly after, changing his tone, he said with some emphasis, "My brother the king of

France has made your emperor a marvellous offer." This he repeated three times. I said, if it were so, he had now done a virtuous part, and kept his professions. After various other topics it grew late. Not a word was said of the queen. After dinner he asked me if I had anything more to say.

All here are satisfied with the treaty of Cambray. It is supposed to have cost this king 800,000 ducats. He is not therefore likely to break it. People here are not very anxious to repeat the dose, as it is not to their taste. At present they seem on good terms with the French. The ambassador has been only once at court with his brother since my arrival. He has been commanded to deliver his message to the council and abstain from communication with the cardinal; at which he was greatly vexed. Various ambassadors are here. The most in favour is the Milanese, on whom the king has spent money. Those who are now in most credit are the dukes of Norfolk and Suffolk. There is not a single person about the king who is not saturated with French money; and though they profess great affection to you, their affection for money is much stronger. I have submitted the proposition to the king respecting the sea being kept free from pirates.

The downfall of the cardinal is complete. He is dismissed from the council, deprived of the chancellorship and constrained to make an inventory of his goods in his own hand, that nothing may be forgotten. It is said that he has acknowledged his faults and presented all his effects to the king. Yesterday the king returned to Greenwich by water secretly, in order to see them, and found them much greater than he expected. He took with him *sa mye* [his darling—Ann Boleyn], her mother and a gentleman of his chamber (Norris). The cardinal, notwithstanding his troubles, has always shown a good face, especially towards the town, but since St Luke's Day all has been changed to sighs and tears night and day. The king, either moved by pity or for fear if he should die the whole extent of his effects would not be found, sent him a ring for his comfort. He has withdrawn with a small attendance to a place ten miles off. They have sent for his son from Paris. People say execrable things of him, all which will be known at this parliament. But those who have raised the storm will not let it abate, not knowing, if he returned to power, what would become of them. The ambassador of France commiserates him most. It was feared the cardinal would get his goods out of the country, and therefore a strict watch was kept at the ports; and the watch insisted on opening the coffers of Cardinal Campeggio, notwithstanding his passport, and, on his refusal, broke open the locks. He said they had done him great wrong to suppose that he could be corrupted by the cardinal, since he had been proof against the innumerable presents offered him by the king.

The chancellor's seal has remained in the hands of the duke of Norfolk till this morning, when it was transferred to Sir Thomas More. Everyone is delighted at his promotion, because he is an upright and learned man and a good servant of the queen. He was chancellor of Lancaster, an office now conferred on Fitzwilliam. Richard Pace, a faithful servant of your majesty, whom the cardinal had kept in prison for two years, as well in the tower of London as in a monastery (Syon House), is set at liberty. Unless his mind should again become unsettled, it is thought he will rise in higher favour at court than ever.

Of the king's affair there is nothing new to communicate, except what the bishop of London has told me, that Dr Stokesley had been sent to France to consult the doctors of Paris. The queen begs your majesty will send some respectable person there to do the same, for without some definitive sentence the king will remain obstinate in his opinions. She thinks that delay will be more dangerous than profitable, and therefore we have thought it desirable not to consent to the postponement demanded. To avoid creating suspicion in the mind of the king, she thinks I had better cease to visit her, but she will provide means for my speaking with her in private. (London, 25 October 1529)

PS: Two days after I had written the above, the cardinal was definitively condemned by the council, declared a rebel and guilty of high treason for having obtained a legatine bull, whereby he had conferred many benefices in the king's patronage. He has been deprived of his dignities, his goods confiscated, and himself sentenced to prison until the king shall decide. This he will not find easy of digestion, but worse remains behind.

Du Bellay to Montmorency

Not much has happened since my letters of the 23rd. After the cardinal had been deprived of the seal and all his goods placed in the king's hands, which are valued at 500,000 crowns, he was ordered to retire to an episcopal mansion, eight leagues hence, to await the king's pleasure. Norfolk has been made chief of the council—and in his absence Suffolk, who has had his mules—and Master More, chancellor, leaving the chancery of Lancaster to Master Feuvillem (Fitzwilliam). They are beginning to assemble for the parliament from all parts of the country, during which the king will occupy the house which belonged to the cardinal. He is coming to see it today to arrange for his residence. I think the king will leave him York, with a portion of his goods, and not treat him worse. If it be so, and if these lords do not agree, as I expect they will not, it is not improbable that he will regain his authority, so I think it will not be bad policy to grant his request, which in no case can do harm. I forbear to urge again my recall, feeling sure that you have done your best for me; but I am astonished that since I began to urge it, you have given me no answer. (London, 27 October 1529)

Cardinal Wolsey

Bill of indictment preferred by Chr. Hales, attorney general, against Cardinal Wolsey, on the 9th October, 21 Henry VIII, at Westminster, for having procured bulls from Clement VII to make himself legate, contrary to the statute of 16 Richard II; which bulls he published at Westminster, 28th August, 15 Henry VIII, and thereupon assumed and exercised the office of legate; by virtue of which, on 27th July, 21 Henry VIII, he conferred upon James Gorton, clerk, the parish church of Stoke Gylford, Surrey, Winchester diocese, void by the death of Andrew Swynno, although Robert, prior of St Pancras, Lewes, was the true patron. He also caused the wills of various persons dying in other dioceses than his own to be proved before his commissioners, instituted legatine visitations and procured for himself surreptitiously several large pensions from various abbots by virtue of his legatine authority. He was accordingly attached, and the sheriff was commanded to produce him in the king's bench on Saturday after the month of Michaelmas.

On that day John Scuse and Chr. Genney produced a writ, by virtue of which they were admitted attornies for the cardinal, who appointed them as such on the 27th October. They pleaded on the cardinal's behalf that he did not know the obtaining of the bulls to be in contempt and prejudice of the king, or against any statute of provisors, but threw himself upon the king's mercy. Judgement was ultimately given that the cardinal should be out of the king's protection, and forfeit to the king all his lands and goods.

Another bill of indictment, similar to the preceding in all respects, except in the undermentioned particulars, was preferred by Chr. Hales, attorney general, on the 20th October, 21 Henry VIII.

By virtue of his legatine authority, Wolsey had, on the

2nd December, 15 Henry VIII, conferred the parish church of Galbye, Leicestershire, Lincoln diocese, void by the death of Richard Woderoffe, on John Alyn LLD, now archbishop of Dublin, although the master and brethren of the hospital of Burton St Lazar, Leicestershire, were the true patrons.

Oxford

Bill in parliament in behalf of the mayor and corporation of the town of Oxford to protect them from the jurisdiction of the university, whose powers have been made more arbitrary by the liberties granted to them at Wolsey's suit, by patent of 1st April, 18 Henry VIII. This patent the commissioners pray may be cancelled.

Campeggio to Salviati

I did not cross the sea till the 26th ult., owing to the various hindrances which met me between London and Dover. At Boulogne I received your letters of 25th September, so that it was impossible for me to speak to the king of England respecting the affairs of Hungary and Germany, but I had done my best in that matter before my departure. A gentleman of the king's crossed the sea in my company who was going to King Ferdinand; I suppose on this account, as the king is disposed to assist in extinguishing this conflagration.

Last evening I arrived at Paris. The king (Francis) is expected here every day. Today I have received yours of 17th August and 2nd September, with the breves for my recall, which travelled from here to Flanders and have been returned hither. I have not yet seen the pope's nuncios. The bearer is Thaddeus, who is proceeding from England to Rome.

Immediately after my departure from London, the designs against the cardinal of York commenced to develop with great violence, so that before I crossed the sea I learned they had deprived him of the seal, and of the management of all affairs and of a great part of his servants; and an inquiry was being made respecting his moneys and other possessions, with very evident signs of his tending to ruin. He has done nothing in the past, so far as ecclesiastical matters are concerned, to merit such disgrace; and therefore, it may be thought, his majesty will not go to extremes but act considerately in this matter, as he is accustomed to do in all his actions. (Paris, 5 November 1529)

News

Extract from a letter written by Erasmus Mercader to Juan Piquer about the 13th November:

The cardinal of England fell by a turn of fortune. He has been deprived of all his offices, and all his goods are taken. They are worth 600,000 angelots, besides what he has spent in building (*en carpentear*) houses and castles, which was more than 300,000 angelots. He is said also to have lent 500,000 angelots without the king's knowledge to the Count Veyda (the waywode), who has lost them to the captains of the Turk, thereby encouraging him to come to Hungary. In France, the goods of all the treasurers have been confiscated for their oppression of the people.

For Thos Cardinal Archbishop of York

Protection during pleasure. By a judgement in the court of king's bench, the cardinal was placed out of the king's protection, on Saturday after a month of Michaelmas last, for various offences against the crown and the statute of provisors, 16 Richard II. (Westminster, 18 November, 21 Henry VIII)

Cardinal Wolsey

Articles against Cardinal Wolsey by the lords (1 December 1529):

1   For obtaining legatine authority in England, to the injury of the king's prerogative and the immunity possessed by the crown for 200 years.

2   For making a treaty with the French king for the pope without the king's knowledge, the king not being named therein, and binding the said French king to abide his award if any controversy arose upon it.

3   For having, when in France, commissioned Sir Gregory Casale, in the king's name, to conclude a treaty with the duke of Ferrara without any warrant from the king.

4   For having in divers letters and instructions to foreign parts used the expression, "the king and I", "I would ye should do thus", and "the king and I give unto you our hearty thanks", using himself more like a fellow to your highness than a subject.

5   For having caused his servants to be sworn only to himself, when it has been the custom for noblemen to swear their households first to be true to the king.

6   For having endangered the king's person in that he, when he knew himself to have the foul and contagious disease of the great pox broken out upon him in divers places of his body, came daily to your grace, rowning in your ear and blowing upon your most noble grace with his perilous and infective breath; and when he was healed, he made the king believe that it was only an imposthume in his head.

7   For giving away as legate divers benefices, both spiritual and temporal.

8   For making ambassadors come first to him alone, so that it may be suspected he instructed them after his own pleasure, contrary to the king's command.

9   For causing all manner of letters to the king from beyond sea to be sent to him first, so that the king knew nothing except what the cardinal chose to show

him and was compelled to follow his devices. Also when the council have suggested doubts which have been afterwards verified, he, to abuse them, used these words: "I will lay my head that no such thing will happen."

10 For compelling spies to give information to him in the first place.

11 For granting licence under the great seal to export grain after the prohibition for his own profit.

12 For writing to ambassadors abroad, in his own name and without the king's knowledge, and causing them to write again to him, so as to conceal their information.

13 For discouraging the hospitality kept in religious houses, by taking impositions of the heads of those houses for his favour in making abbots and priors and for visitation fees, which is a great cause that there be so many vagabonds, beggars and thieves.

14 For surveying and relating at increased rents the lands of the houses he had suppressed, putting out copyholders or compelling them to pay new fines.

15 For arrogant demeanour in the council chamber, letting no man speak but one or two great personages.

16 For delaying suitors, whom he took pleasure in making attend on him at his own house; so that it has been affirmed ten of the wisest men in England would not be sufficient to order in reasonable time the matters he would retain to himself.

17 For appropriating by his legatine authority the goods of spiritual men when they had any riches, and, when executors remonstrated, putting them in fear by refusing to meddle.

18 For compelling all the ordinaries in England to compound with him that he might not usurp half or the whole of their jurisdiction by prevention, and to extort treasure, for there is never a poor archdeacon in

England but that he paid yearly to him a portion of his living.

19 For shamefully slandering many good religious houses, by which means he suppressed 30, exceeding even the powers given him in his bull, which enabled him only to suppress houses that had not more than six or seven in them. He then caused offices to be found by untrue verdicts that the religious persons had voluntarily abandoned their houses.

20 For examining matters in chancery after judgement had been given on them by the common law, and compelling parties to restore to the opposite party what they had recovered by execution in the common law.

21 For granting injunctions by writ when the parties were never called, nor bills put in against them.

22 For suspending pardons granted by the pope until he had a yearly pension out of them.

23 For putting out many farmers of his lands, and grantees of the archbishopric of York, etc.

24 For inducing houses of religion to promise their elections to him, and obtaining from them so much goods as almost to ruin the houses.

25 For taking from religious houses one twenty-fifth of their livelihood at visitations.

26 For threatening the judges to prevent a decision.

27 For making his son Winter spend 2,700*l.* a year, which he takes to his own use, and gives him only 200*l.* to live on.

28 For violating his promise to the king, when he asked his assent to be legate, not to do anything in prejudice of the king or bishops.

29 For slandering the clergy of England by writing to Rome that they had given themselves *in reprobum sensum.*

30 For appropriating most of the goods of Dr Smith, late bishop of London, Bishop Savage of York, Mr Dalby, archdeacon of Richmond, Dr Tornyers, bishop of Durham, and Dr Fox, bishop of Winchester.

31 For removing into chancery the indictments against his officers for taking 12*d*. in 1*l*. for probation of wills, and rebuking Mr Justice FitzHerbert.

32 For promoting dissension amongst the nobles.

33 For compelling the king's subjects to serve him with carts for carriage, corn and other victual, at the king's prices and under.

34 For keeping great estate at court in the king's absence.

35 His servants have taken cattle and other victuals at as low price as the king's purveyors.

36 For preventing the king's officers from taking wheat, as was the custom, out of the liberty of St Albans.

37 For forbidding persons who had been before him in the Star Chamber to sue to the king for pardon.

38 For committing to the Fleet one Sir John Stanley of Adlington, who married one Lark's daughter, which woman the said lord cardinal kept, and had with her two children; whereupon the said Sir John Stanley, upon displeasure taken in his heart, made himself monk in Westminster, and there died.

39 For interfering with the king's clerk of the market, who, when the king came to St Albans, presented to the household as usual the prices of all manner of victuals within the verge. He was commanded to set the said prices up, according to custom, on the gates of the household, and in the marketplace of St Albans; but Wolsey ordered them to be taken down, though they were sealed with the king's seal, and his own prices set up sealed with his seal. He also would have set the clerk of the market in the stocks.

40 For stamping the cardinal's hat under the king's arms on the coin of groats made at York.

41 For committing to the Fleet Wm Johnson, who had a lease of the parsonage of Crowley from Sir Edw. Jones, clerk, and disputed a claim to that parsonage raised by the dean of Cardinal's College, Oxford, on the ground that it belonged to the parsonage of Chichley, appropriated to the suppressed priory of Tyleford.

42 For issuing an injunction out of chancery to one Martin Docowar, to avoid possession of the manor of Balsall, in Warwickshire, in favour of Sir George Throgmorton, until the matter depending between the prior of St John's and the said Docowar were discussed. The latter has never been called to make answer in chancery.

43 For prohibiting two bishops from visiting the university of Cambridge to prevent the spread of Lutheran heresies.

44 They beg the king to make the cardinal an example. 1st December, 21 Henry VIII.

Signed: T. More, T. Norfolk, Char. Suffolk, Tho. Dorset, H. Exeter, G. Shrewsbury, R. Fitzwater, Jo. Oxenford, H. Northumberland, T. Darcy, T. Rochford, W. Mountjoy, Will. Sandys, William Fitzwilliam, Henry Guldeford, Anthony FitzHerbert, John FitzJames.

Cardinal Wolsey and Thomas Cromwell

Cardinal Wolsey, in his disgrace, employed Cromwell in soliciting his affairs at court, to get his pardon, and thanks him for his care therein in many letters with his own hand.

When he was commanded to York, he desired the king's letters of recommendation to the nobility in the north, which he would have favourably indited, and Mr Secretary to be moved therein, of whom he expects some help for his old deserts, etc.

These letters were so favourably penned that the cardinal, in a letter of the king to Lord Dacres, is called, "Our right trusty and right well beloved the Lord Cardinal, etc."

When Wolsey was at Asher he writes thus to Cromwell: "My fever is somewhat assuaged, and the black humour also. Howbeit, I am entering into the calends of a more dangerous sickness, which is the dropsy, so that if I be not removed to a drier air, and that shortly, there is little hope."

He entreats Cromwell to solicit the king to be gracious to him, and to practise that the Lady Anne may mediate for him.

He styles Cromwell "My only comfort", "My only help", "Mine own good Thomas" and "My only refuge and aid".

He writes to Cromwell that he hopes that for his maintenance, and to do good to his servants and bestow alms (which York will not do), the king (if he take from him Winchester) will allow him a pension out of it:

> For God be my judge, I never thought, and so I was
> assured at the making of my submission, to depart from
> any of my promotions; for the rigour of the law, for any
> offence that can be arrected unto me, deserveth no such
> punishment; and so, trusting in the king's goodness, I am
> come to this point. I hope his grace will consider the same
> accordingly. I have had fair words, but little comfortable
> deeds. Those noblemen did otherwise promise on their
> honours to me, upon trust whereof I made the frank gift
> of mine whole estate.
>
> If it might be possible to retain Winchester, though the
> king had the most part of the profits, etc., or else there
> might be some good sum made for the retention of the
> same.

In another letter Wolsey says:

> As touching the articles laid unto me, whereof a great part
> be untrue, and those which be true are of such sort that by
> the doing of them no malice nor untruth can be justly
> arerued unto me, neither to the prince's person, nor to the
> realm, etc. This may be fitted to the king.
>
> As touching the coin at York with the letters and badges
> in the same, ye may commune with Pawlet, &c. officer of
> the mint, how the usage hath been of the mint.

He complains of the wrong information of the earl of
Northumberland. He thanks Cromwell for getting his pardon and restitution to York sealed. He hopes that the king
(to whom he hath given all his goods and revenues) will
pay his debts, which may be done with the arrearages of
my pension out of France for the year bypast. He entreats
Cromwell to sue that his colleges be preserved, for (saith
he) they are, in a manner, the works of your own hands.

Cromwell wrote to the cardinal on July 12, 1529:

> As touching the process against your grace out of the
> exchequer and all other matters and suits brought against
> you, I have pleaded your pardon, which is allowed in all
> the king's courts, and by the same your grace discharged of
> all manner causes at the king's suit.

Cromwell tells the cardinal that this soliciting his cause
hath been very chargeable to him, and he cannot sustain
it any longer without other respect than he hath had
heretofore:

> I am 1,000*l*. worse than I was when your troubles began. . . .
> As touching your colleges, the king is determined to
> dissolve them, and that new offices shall be found of all the

lands belonging to them newly to intitle his highness, which be already drawn for this purpose. But whether his highness, after the dissolution of them, mean to revive them again, and found them in his own name, I know not. Wherefore I entreat your grace to be content, and let your prince execute his pleasure.

Rafe Sadler wrote to the cardinal that "his Master [i.e. Cromwell] hath accepted his token, which yet was not so great a reward as he expected (the cardinal alleged his necessity, etc.).

Cromwell wrote to the cardinal:

The king hath received his letters, and is very sorry that he is in such necessity, yet that, for relief, his majesty hath deferred it till he speak with his council. The duke of Norfolk promiseth you his best aid, but he willeth you for the present to be content, and not much to molest the king (concerning payment of your debts etc.) for, as he supposeth, the time is not meet for it. The king showed me how it is come to his knowledge that your grace should have certain words of him and other noblemen unto my lord of Norfolk since the time of your adversities, which words should sound to make sedition betwixt him and my lord of Norfolk.

Mr Page received your letter directed unto my Lady Anne, and delivered the same. There is yet no answer. She gave kind words, but will not promise to speak to the king for you.

Certain doctors of both the universities are here for the suppression of the Lutheran opinions. The king's highness hath caused the said doctors at divers times assemble, and hath communed with them. The fame is that Luther is departed this life. I would he had never been born.

Cromwell entreats Wolsey to have patience:

> There shall be some offices sent into York and
> Nottinghamshire to be found of your lands belonging to
> your archbishopric. This will be very displeasant to you,
> but it is best to suffer it, for, if they should not be found,
> you could not hold your bishopric quiet, notwithstanding
> your pardon; for your restitution made by your pardon is
> clearly void, for that the king did restitute your grace
> before he was entitled by matter of record. When these
> offices shall be found, your pardon shall be good and stand
> in perfect effect.

He tells him that his modest behaviour and humility hath
gained him the love and good report of the country where
he now lives, and also in the court, yet his enemies deprave
all. "Sir, some there be that do allege that your grace doth
keep too great a house and family. Have a respect, and
refrain, etc."

Cromwell wrote to the cardinal in August 1529:

> I am informed your grace hath me in some diffidence, as
> if I did dissemble with you, or procure anything contrary
> to your profit and honour. I much muse that your grace
> should so think, or report it secretly, considering the pains
> I have taken, etc. Wherefore I beseech you to speak
> without feigning if you have such conceit, that I may
> clear myself. I reckoned that your grace would have
> written plainly unto me of such thing, rather than secretly
> to have misreported me, etc. But I shall bear your grace
> no less good will, etc. Let God judge between us. Truly
> your grace in some things overshooteth yourself; there is
> reg(ard) to be given what things ye utter, and to whom,
> etc.

Cromwell seemed to keep certain scholars in Cambridge, for he entreats the cardinal to prefer them to benefices which should fall in his archbishopric.

The cardinal strives to clear himself to Cromwell, protesting that he suspects him not, and that may appear by his deeds, for that he useth no man's help nor counsel but his. Indeed, report hath been made to him that Cromwell hath not done him so good offices as he might concerning his colleges and his archbishopric; but he hath not believed them, yet he hath asked of their common friends how Cromwell hath behaved himself towards him, and, to his great comfort, hath found him faithful, etc. Therefore he beseecheth him with weeping tears to continue steadfast, and give no credit to "the false suggestions of such as would sow variance between us, and so leave me destitute of all help, etc." (October 1529)

None dares speak to the king on his part for fear of Madame Anne's displeasure.

The cardinal takes the suppressing and dismembering of his colleges very heavily. He heartily and earnestly solicits Cromwell and others to aid the said colleges, that what the pope and the king have done and confirmed may not be made void, which thing should be against all laws of God and man.

He writes to the king "humbly and on my knees with weeping eyes to recommend unto your excellent charity and goodness the poor college of Oxford". (This letter was to be presented by the dean and canons thereof, October 1529)

Sir Thomas More

To the treasurer and barons of the exchequer, the general surveyor of lands, the auditors of the accounts of the Hanaper of Chancery, of the chief butler, and others.

Warrant to allow to Sir Thos More, as lord chancellor, the yearly sum of 142*l*. 15*s*. from 25 October, 21 Henry

VIII; and for his attendance in the Star Chambers, 200*l*. a year. Also the chief butler is to allow him 64*l*. a year for the price of 12 tuns of wine; and the keeper of the great wardrobe, 16*l*. a year for wax. (Westminster, 2 December, 21 Henry VIII)

Erasmus to Francis, treasurer of Besançon
Three months ago sent a servant to England to inquire what truth there was in the rumour that the great cardinal of England had been thrown into prison, and was even in danger of his life. Oh, the slippery turns of this world! (Fribourg, 10 December 1529)

∘⊸⊰✕⊱⊶∘

Wolsey died in the following year, before the king's judgement on him was passed. Within two years, Henry VIII declared himself supreme head of the Church in England, and thus split the English Church from the Church of Rome. Able, then, to satisfy his own cause, he divorced Katherine of Aragon and married Anne Boleyn. Katherine died in 1535. Anne was convicted of incest, adultery and high treason and executed in 1536.

∘⊸⊰✕⊱⊶∘

Other titles in the series

Escape from Germany, 1939–45

*"It is quite certain that, apart from the microphone, no evidence what-
ever had been found to show a tunnel was being dug, yet in the
four and-a-half months from the commencement of the tunnel campaign, more than 166 tons of sand had been excavated from three
tunnels and hidden in a compound only a mile in circumference which
was constantly patrolled and inspected by Germans."*

Backdrop
The history of Air Force captivity in Germany began on 3
September 1939, the day Britain declared war on Germany. On the
same day, a New Zealand officer was shot down over the North Sea
and was subsequently taken prisoner. By December 1939, the
numbers of those captured had grown, and the Germans began
to segregate Air Force prisoners, housing them in special camps.

The Book
Of the 10,000 British airmen held as prisoners-of-war by the
Germans during World War II, less than 30 successfully managed
to find their way back to Britain or to a neutral country. After
1945, many escapers and PoWs were interviewed, and a file was
built up of their various experiences. This file was kept secret for
nearly 40 years (despite the fact that several famous films were
made about these escapes), as it was thought to contain evidence
of enterprise and resilience that could still be useful to an enemy.
Now "uncovered" for the public to read, this book contains the
true and often incredible stories of the heroic attempts of these
men to escape. Drawn from the narratives of the men themselves,
it includes such remarkable stories as "The Trojan Horse"—a
hollow vaulting horse that was used to disguise a tunnel
entrance—and the persistent and ingenious attempts to escape
made from camps such as the formidable Colditz.

ISBN 0 11 702459 7   Price £6.99

War in the Falklands, 1982

"On 22 March 1982 [10 days before the invasion], the Ministry of Foreign Affairs expressed concern at news of an insult to the Argentine flag at the LADE (Argentine Air Force airline) office in Port Stanley. The Governor reported that on the night of 20/21 March the LADE office had been entered, apparently by someone using a key. A Union flag had been placed over the Argentine flag there and 'Tit for tat, you buggers' written in tooth-paste on a desk. In a later incident, during the night of 22/23 March, 'UK OK' was written on two external windows of the LADE office."

Backdrop
Since 1832, Britain has claimed sovereignty over the Falkland Islands in the South Atlantic. On 2 April 1982 Argentina invaded the Falklands and took possession of Port Stanley.

The Book
How did Britain come to have sovereignty over a small group of islands over 8,000 miles away? What were the events leading up to the Argentine invasion, and why was Britain caught so unprepared? What were the logistical problems involved in mounting a campaign to retake these islands? And how were feel-ings expressed about this extraordinary event?

These are just some of the issues which are dealt with by the archive material in this uncovered edition. Starting with the offi-cial government history of the Falkland Islands (from 1592, when the islands were first sighted), the book then gives the full text of Lord Franks' report, who was appointed in 1982 to investigate the events leading up to the invasion, and to review the way in which the Government discharged its responsibilities. A full description of the operation as submitted to Parliament is included, and also the text of some famous debates in the House of Commons during this turbulent period, featuring interchanges between Margaret Thatcher and the leaders of the other parties.

ISBN 0 11 702458 9   Price £6.99

King Guezo of Dahomey, 1850–52

"Retiring to our seats, the King insisted on our viewing the place of sacrifice. Immediately under the royal canopy were six or eight executioners, armed with large knives, grinning horribly; the mob now armed with clubs and branches, yelled furiously, calling upon the King to 'feed them – they were hungry'. . . When it was all over, at 3 pm, we were permitted to retire. At the foot of the ladder in the boats and baskets lay the bleeding heads. It is my duty to describe; I leave exposition to the reader."

Backdrop

In 1807, the British Parliament outlawed the trade in slaves, followed in 1833 by an Act to abolish the institution of slavery. However, in 1850, the slave trade was alive and well on the west coast of Africa.

The Book

The fact that Africans were still being sold into slavery in the mid-19th century was partly due to the reluctance of both the merchants and the African chiefs to desist. King Guezo was one of these African chiefs who profited by selling captives taken during tribal wars. Although he was very friendly towards the British, counting Queen Victoria as one of his most revered friends, he was reluctant to give up his war-like habits. With 18,000 royal wives, an army composed in part of 3,000 Amazon women, and a warrior-like reputation to maintain, he could see little attraction in farming as an alternative lifestyle. For entertainment, he would regularly indulge in human sacrifice.

Lord Palmerston was the Foreign Secretary who charged the British Consul in west Africa with the unenviable task of persuading the African chiefs to give up their lucrative trade. Just how the British managed to coerce the chiefs into abandoning this practice is revealed in fresh and fascinating detail by these contemporary despatches. They provide an astonishing glimpse of the customs and way of life in Africa some 150 years ago, as told by the people who were there.

ISBN 0 11 702460 0   Price £6.99

War 1939: Dealing with Adolf Hitler

"Herr Hitler asserted that I did not care how many Germans were being slaughtered in Poland. This gratuitous impugnment of the humanity of His Majesty's Government and of myself provoked a heated retort on my part and the remainder of the interview was of a somewhat stormy character."

The Backdrop
As he presided over the rebuilding of a Germany shattered and humiliated after World War I, opinion regarding Hitler and his intentions was divided and the question of whether his ultimate aim was military domination by no means certain.

The Book
Sir Nevile Henderson, the British ambassador in Berlin in 1939, describes here, in his report to Parliament, the failure of his mission and the events leading up to the outbreak of war. He tells of his attempts to deal with both Hitler and von Ribbentrop to maintain peace and gives an account of the changes in German foreign policy regarding Poland. The second part of the book contains documents concerning German-Polish relations up to September 1939.

ISBN 0 11 702411 2   Price £6.99

D Day to VE Day: General Eisenhower's Report, 1944–45

"During the spring of 1945, as the sky grew darker over Germany, the Nazi leaders had struggled desperately, by every means in their power, to whip their people into a last supreme effort to stave off defeat, hoping against hope that it would be possible, if only they could hold out long enough, to save the day by dividing the Allies. Blinded as they were by their own terror and hatred of 'Bolshevism', they were incapable of understanding the strength of the bond of common interest existing between Britain, the United States and the Soviet Union."

Backdrop

In 1944 the Allies were poised to launch an attack against Hitler's German war machine. The planning and timing were crucial. In February, General Eisenhower was appointed Supreme Commander of the Allied Operations in Europe.

The Book

The book is Dwight D. Eisenhower's personal account of the Allied invasion of Europe, from the preparations for the D-Day landings in Normandy, France, to the final assault across Germany. He presents a story of a far more arduous struggle than is commonly portrayed against an enemy whose tenacity he admired and whose skills he feared. It is a tactical account of his understanding of enemy manoeuvres, and his attempts to counter their actions. The formality of the report is coloured by many personal touches, and the reader senses Eisenhower's growing determination to complete the task. Hindsight would have had the general take more notice of Russian activity, but that this was not obvious to him is one of the fascinations of such a contemporary document.

ISBN 0 11 702451 1   Price £6.99

Bloody Sunday, 1972: Lord Widgery's Report

"No order and no training can ensure that a soldier will always act wisely, as well as bravely and with initiative. The individual soldier ought not to have to bear the burden of deciding whether to open fire in confusion such as prevailed on 30 January. In the conditions prevailing in Northern Ireland, however, this is often inescapable."

Backdrop

Northern Ireland forms part of the United Kingdom, and the Protestant majority of its population generally supports political union with Great Britain. However, many of the Roman Catholic minority would prefer union with the Republic of Ireland. This division has sparked much of the conflict between the two communities. In 1969, a British Army peace-keeping force was established in Northern Ireland.

The Book

On Sunday 30 January 1972, a protest march organised by the Northern Ireland Civil Rights Association took place in Londonderry, Northern Ireland, in the area of the Bogside and Creggan Estate. During the afternoon of that march, 13 civilians were killed by British soldiers, and another 13 were injured. As a result, a tribunal was appointed to inquire into the events which led up to this tragic loss of life. Heading the inquiry was Lord Widgery. This uncovered edition is the text of his report.

ISBN 0 11 702405 8   Price £6.99

The Irish Uprising, 1914–21: Papers from the British Parliamentary Archive

"Captain Bowen-Colthurst adopted the extraordinary, and indeed almost meaningless, course of taking Mr Sheehy Skeffington with him as a hostage' He had no right to take Mr Sheehy Skeffington out of the custody of the guard for this or any other purpose, and he asked no one's leave to do so. . . . Before they left the barracks Mr Sheehy Skeffington's hands were tied behind his back and Captain Bowen-Colthurst called upon him to say his prayers. Upon Mr Sheehy Skeffington refusing to do so Captain Bowen-Colthurst ordered the men of his party to take their hats off and himself uttered a prayer, the words of it being: 'O Lord God, if it shall please thee to take away the life of this man, forgive him for Christ's sake.'"

Backdrop
In 1914 it was still the case that the whole of Ireland was part of Great Britain, under the dominion of the King, and Irish constituencies were represented in the British Parliament.

The Book
This book contains five remarkable documents published by the British Government between 1914 and 1921, relating to the events leading up to the partition of Ireland in 1921. In the first, a report is made into the shooting of civilians following a landing of arms at Howth outside Dublin. The second is of the papers discovered relating to the activities of Sinn Fein and particularly of Sir Roger Casement. The third is the government inquiry into the Easter Rising of 1916. The fourth describes the treatment of three journalists by the British Army shortly after the uprising, and the last is an exchange of correspondence between Eamon de Valera and David Lloyd George prior to the Anglo-Irish Treaty of 1921.

ISBN 0 11 702415 5   Price £6.99

The Siege of the Peking Embassy, 1900

"I cannot conclude this despatch without saying a word of praise respecting the ladies of all nationalities who so ably and devotedly assisted the defence, notwithstanding the terrible shadow which at all times hung over the legation—a shadow which the never-ceasing rattle of musketry and crash of round shot and shell and the diminishing number of defenders rendered ever present. They behaved with infinite patience and cheerfulness, helping personally in the hospital or, in making sandbags and bandages, and in assisting in every possible way the work of defence. Especially commended are two young ladies—Miss Myers and Miss Daisy Brazier—who daily filtered the water for the hospital, in tropical heat, and carried it with bullets whistling and shells bursting in the trees overhead." Sir Claude MacDonald

Backdrop
The Boxer movement in China was a secret society which preached hatred of foreigners. By the spring of 1900, this movement was out of control. On 9 June, the Boxers launched their first attack against foreign property in Peking by burning down the racecourse. On 19 June, all foreigners were ordered to evacuate Peking within 24 hours. The order was not complied with.

The Book
As events worsened for the diplomats and their families in Peking, Sir Claude MacDonald, the British ambassador, wired the Admiralty in Taku to request the immediate despatch of a relief force. Just how that relief force fared, and how the hundreds of diplomats and their families who were stranded inside the Legation buildings coped with the rigours of the siege, are the subject of the diplomatic papers presented in this book. The central part of the story is the gripping diary of events kept by Sir Claude MacDonald.

ISBN 0 11 702456 2   Price £6.99